How to plan
a happy and
financially
secure
retirement

the
golden
years

Jamie Nemtsas
and Drew Meredith

MAJOR
STREET

MAJOR STREET

First published in 2024 by Major Street Publishing Pty Ltd
info@majorstreet.com.au | majorstreet.com.au

A catalogue record for this book is available from the National Library of Australia

Printed book ISBN: 978-1-923186-01-9
Ebook ISBN: 978-1-923186-02-6

Cover design by Typography Studio
Internal design by Production Works

10 9 8 7 6 5 4 3 2 1

Contents

Preface

Retirement is supposed to be the most enjoyable and relaxing period of your life. Most of us spend our entire lives working towards the goal of an independent and exciting retirement. We squirrel money away every month, pay off our mortgages as fast as we can and make sure we have enough insurance in place in case it all goes wrong. We invest, trade and take risks in the hope of retiring and enjoying the same lifestyle as we did in our working lives. Unfortunately, retirement isn't always what it's cracked up to be or what we see in the stock images of grey-haired couples drinking cocktails on a beach.

Being career financial advisers, we have been in the privileged position of seeing how thousands of people have navigated retirement from both a financial and lifestyle perspective. From holding the hand of a widowed client whose husband passed away shortly after retiring, to touring aged care homes, to advising those who have more than enough money but are scared to spend it, we have seen it all. And, to be frank, far too many people are not enjoying their retirement to the level that they should, particularly given how hard they have worked during their lives.

It would be an understatement to say that the financial services industry has ignored retirees for the last few decades.

Industry super funds have millions of members but are, by their nature, tilted towards younger, contributing members. Then there are financial advisers, the vast majority of whom are 'generalists' and thus unable or unwilling to meet the unique needs of the hundreds of thousands of people entering retirement each year. And the level of digestible financial education available to retirees pales in comparison to the volume of share-trading, cryptocurrency and property podcasts, blogs and magazines.

The idea to write this book came from a chat in our shared office at Wattle Partners. Each week, we take time to reflect, over a drink, on the conversations we have had with clients and think about what retirement means to us personally and our families. Having spent close to 40 years (combined, of course) advising people on their retirement, we see an incredible need for a dedicated retirement resource. In this book, we hope to provide you with an insight into some of the things, both expected and unexpected, that can take your retirement from 'ho-hum' to the 'golden years' – and all for less than $35.

So many people think that they or their families are different, but we can assure you that we have seen everything, and whatever your situation, you are not alone. This book draws from thousands of meetings we have had with people over the years and includes case studies to highlight best-case scenarios or common pitfalls to avoid. Of course, this book is no substitute for personal financial advice, but hopefully it will be a good starting point for you.

We have also distilled some of our most impactful conversations into our 'golden rules', which apply both to the way you invest your money and the way you live your life in retirement. These are the rules that we follow in our own lives and which we hope will put you on the right path.

We must thank Jon Glass for his involvement and insights into the lifestyle and mental challenges that come with retirement, and both Penny Pryor and James Dunn, whose support made this book possible.

Ultimately, if you take anything from this book, we hope it is that there is no single right way to approach retirement – it depends solely on what you value and where you find the most joy.

Jamie Nemtsas and Drew Meredith
February 2024

1

The long road that is retirement

Simon and Yoshi have been friends since they boarded together at high school. However, that's over 40 years ago now, and lately the discussions when they catch up have revolved around their retirement plans. They are both aged 65 and their spouses, Jan and Jane, are both aged 63. Simon runs a mechanical engineering company and Yoshi is a high-performance executive coach.

Simon has just inherited over $1 million after his father passed away and, along with a superannuation fund of just over $1 million, is in a very strong financial position for his retirement. He is still working full time but plans to completely retire in just over 12 months. Having focused heavily on his career for the last 20 years, Simon is looking forward to having the time and money to travel overseas, and to renovate and extend the family home, two things that have been on his to-do list for years. Jan, Simon's wife, is not sure what she wants to do and is still very much enjoying her role as principal of their local primary school. Their two adult children have partners, but they have no grandchildren yet.

Yoshi, on the other hand, has already scaled back his work hours and intends to continue working in some form into his early seventies, transitioning slowly into retirement. He has seen first-hand the search for meaning that can happen when people who have tied their self-worth to their career retire. He has been discussing his plans with Jane, a teacher, for many years now and they are both on the same page. They are also in a decent financial position, with close to $950,000 combined in super, and will be able to take a transition to retirement pension to draw down on this balance slowly. Yoshi and Jane have strong family connections with their three children and two grandchildren. They are very active in the community, are members of the local tennis club and run a dog rescue charity together.

Five years on, Simon and Yoshi might now be the same age (70), but they are in very different positions both financially and emotionally.

Yoshi's retirement is pretty much on track. He is still working, but only one day a week, and taking a transition-to-retirement pension. His wife is also teaching casually about one day a week and drawing a small pension from their fund. These income sources combined are giving them enough to live on while not drawing down their capital balance too much. Their charity work continues to keep them busy, and they have also joined a bushwalking club. They have taken a couple of short trips overseas while they are still in relatively good health.

Simon's story is a little different. The first thing he and Jan did once they retired was take a six-month holiday to Europe. They had an amazing time, and when they got back they headed straight into renovating their home. This, combined with an extension and a studio in the backyard, ended up costing them a lot more than they originally intended. It also took them a lot longer, with the whole project only being completed six months ago. They are now wondering whether they will have to sell to realise the value and inject it back into superannuation. This has, understandably, hit Simon for six emotionally, and after the initial euphoria of retirement and seemingly unlimited money and spare time, he is struggling a little. Fortunately, he is due for a catch-up with Yoshi, who has some ideas he hopes to share with Simon around retirement coaching.

The five stages of retirement

Retirement is a very long road. While a lot of focus is placed on the importance of being financially prepared for retirement – and the rest of this book will go into detail about some of the financial issues you might face – this isn't the only thing you should be thinking about leading up to, and entering into, retirement.

It is helpful to break down retirement into five basic stages. You may not experience all of these, but knowing what they are can help you prepare.

Stage 1: 'pretirement'

As you head into your late fifties – or even earlier, if you're lucky – you should really start to think about when you want to retire and how you are going to go about doing it. Your finances and whether you will have enough to sustain your desired income in retirement (which we go into much more detail about in Chapter 3) is one thing, but you also need to be having discussions with your spouse about their retirement intentions. For example, Yoshi and Jane have been talking about their retirement plans since their early fifties. Note that you don't have to retire at the same time.

If you don't have a spouse, that makes some decisions easier, but you will also only have the one superannuation account to rely on.

Retirement intentions

There are 4.1 million retirees in Australia. The average age at retirement of all retirees is 56.3 years (or 59.3 years for men and 54 years for women). However, the average age people intend to retire is 65.5 years – 66 years for men and 64.9 years for women.

Stage 2: the honeymoon period

When you first stop working, it may seem like you have one long holiday stretching out in front of you. You probably have trips planned, whether they are overseas cruises or caravanning holidays in Australia. And when you return from those trips, there is all that gardening to get stuck into, or golf, or whatever hobby you neglected during your working life.

During those early months and years, you can really feel like you've found the sense of freedom that you may have been missing in your career. This is often to referred to as the 'honeymoon period' of retirement. Unfortunately, for most people, this sense of euphoria doesn't last forever.

Stage 3: disenchantment

The end of the honeymoon period generally brings about a period of disenchantment. Travelling is fun, but it is also expensive and eats into your superannuation funds. This is doubly concerning when you are no longer earning an income.

Also, instead of having all that free time to work on things you love, you may instead get roped into minding grandkids or fur babies. Or perhaps your volunteer activities may be using up more of your time than you anticipated. You may end up having almost as many constraints on your time as you did when you were working.

Speaking of work, many people – especially high-powered executives – also miss the sense of identity their careers gave them, or they may just miss the water-cooler conversation and social interaction they got in the office.

This is the phase that Simon found himself in five years after he finished working.

Stage 4: reorientation

To move on from the disenchantment phase, you need to snap yourself out of the fug and get down to some serious planning. This involves setting more realistic goals for how you want to spend both your time and money in retirement. You may also need to set some boundaries for things like babysitting or volunteer work. You could tell your children you will only babysit on certain days of the week, for example. If you still want to travel, you need to work out what you can afford both financially and physically.

You need to recalibrate your mindset so you can be grateful for the life you have and not be hankering after the life you've lost. We expect that Yoshi will be able to help Simon do this, but Simon will also need to speak to some experts to assist him with this journey.

Stage 5: stability

Finally, following a period of reorientation, you are set for a retirement life of stability. However, while your finances and plans are more stable, this can also be when the body starts acting up. The aches and pains become more prevalent, and you don't have the energy you used to have (see the statistics in the panel below), although hopefully you have more peace of mind.

It's during this period of stability that you really need to make sure you have the appropriate succession plans in place for transferring wealth to your spouse or younger generations. Chapter 5 explores these difficult issues more deeply. Having your affairs in order before this happens greatly reduces the shock and strain on the surviving partner. And if you haven't thought or planned about it yet, aged care plans should also be a priority.

Health and age

As Figure 1.1 highlights, you are far more likely to have at least one, if not two, chronic health conditions over age 60.

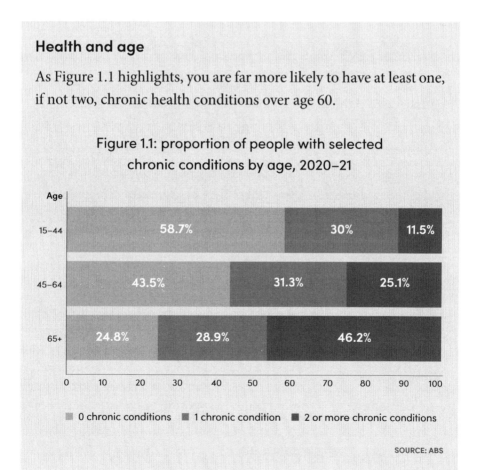

Figure 1.1: proportion of people with selected chronic conditions by age, 2020–21

Age	0 chronic conditions	1 chronic condition	2 or more chronic conditions
15–44	58.7%	30%	11.5%
45–64	43.5%	31.3%	25.1%
65+	24.8%	28.9%	46.2%

■ 0 chronic conditions   ■ 1 chronic condition   ■ 2 or more chronic conditions

SOURCE: ABS

The super system versus a retirement system

Australia has a superannuation system that is the envy of much of the modern world, but it is very much set up for accumulation. The system takes a burden off government by encouraging and enforcing Australians to save for their own retirement via the superannuation guarantee. It is relatively young at just over 30 years old and has generally not focused on retirees, instead emphasising maximising balances until you retire.

It took legislative change and the introduction of the retirement income covenant, which only occurred very recently, for Australia's largest superannuation funds to focus on providing fit-for-purpose retirement income products for members. In Chapter 6 we examine the different ways you can access your superannuation funds and how to draw an income in retirement.

Not only does retirement require a different type of product, but it also requires a different mindset when it comes to investment. For most of your accumulation years, you (or your superannuation fund on your behalf) will be investing for growth – that is, investing in assets like shares that have the potential to outperform cash and/or inflation over the longer term. The average annual return of Australian shares, for example, over the 33 years from 1 August 1970 until end of July 2023 was 9.9 per cent. But with those higher returns comes greater risk and, in any year, the stock market can fall by 5, 10, 15 per cent or more. That's fine if you've got another 20 years to make up those losses, but it is concerning if you've just entered your retirement. This was the case for many new retirees in the wake of the global financial crisis (GFC), and some found themselves forced back to work because of the dint in their retirement kitty.

Hence, you need to take a more conservative approach to investing in your retirement with a much bigger focus on income-producing assets and asset classes. As Table 1.1 shows, while the annual average return of income-producing assets such as Australian bonds and cash is lower than that for growth assets, it is still robust.

Table 1.1: annual average return of various asset classes since 1 August 1970

Asset class	Annual average return since 1 August 1970
Australian shares	9.9% p.a.
International shares	10.4% p.a.
US shares	12.2% p.a.
Australian bonds	7.6% p.a.
Cash	7.4% p.a.

SOURCE: VANGUARD DIGITAL INDEX CHART. DATA AS AT END JULY 2023

Chapter 7 examines ideal asset allocation strategies for retirees and different risk approaches. Along with investing in appropriate asset classes for your life stage, it's also very important to understand your risk profile and what level of uncertainty you are comfortable with around investments. This is sometimes called the 'sleep at night' test, meaning that there is no point investing in an asset with a high growth profile if it keeps you up worrying about it.

What is the retirement income covenant?

The Morrison Government introduced legislation for a retirement income covenant that was designed 'to give retirees the confidence to spend their superannuation savings, while enabling choice and competition in the retirement phase of superannuation' in 2021.

The legislation requires superannuation trustees of funds regulated by the Australian Prudential Regulation Authority (APRA) to have a retirement income strategy that outlined how they planned to assist their members in retirement. It does not apply to self-managed superannuation funds (SMSFs). Since 1 July 2022 superannuation funds are required to formulate a retirement income strategy and publish a summary of the strategy on their website. Where it sits on a super fund's website varies: it could be in their 'About us' section, their 'Retirement section' or their 'Forms and documents' section.

But these large funds still have work to do according to a joint review in 2023 by APRA and the Australian Securities and Investments Commission (ASIC). APRA said that while some funds had gotten off to a good start overall, there was insufficient urgency. The regulators called on trustees to step up and deliver well-considered strategies and action to support members in retirement.

Plan your life as well as your finances

This book examines how to best position yourself financially to enjoy your golden years of retirement. It looks at the various issues of how much is enough, what kinds of superannuation funds exist, how to get estate planning right and how to make appropriate investment allocations. However, the focus on financial preparations for retirement can cause so many other things to be overlooked, and it is just as important to plan out your retirement in terms of how you want to spend your days and what you want to achieve.

What is my passion or purpose?

To help you make your way down the long and sometimes winding road of retirement, it is useful to start with a passion or purpose. What haven't you been able to do while you have been working and hope to be able to do more of now? This could be golf, exercise, education, volunteering or any number of pastimes, but you need to find at least one thing that you think will give you meaning in your retirement. This is especially the case if you have derived much of your meaning and self-worth from your career, and even doubly so for very senior executives who are accustomed to power.

You might decide that having been sitting behind a desk for most of your life, you want to do something more physical in your retirement. Perhaps you want to garden more or grow your own produce. Perhaps you want to volunteer or set up your own charity, like Yoshi and Jane did in our example at the beginning of this chapter.

In working out what your passion is, it's important to consider what you will miss the most from your working life. If you think you'll miss the banter at the water cooler, then maybe your passion needs to incorporate a lot of social interaction. If you think you'll miss all the things you learn while on the job, then your purpose might want to include an education aspect.

There is no right or wrong purpose, and it can also change over time. You might not be able to continue to garden into your eighties, and so your purpose could then shift to educating others about gardening as your physical health declines. If you decide helping with your grandchildren is your purpose, then that will change over time as they grow up and mature as well.

Once you've worked out one or two purposes or passions, it is helpful to set goals.

Short-term goals

There's nothing wrong with wanting to go on a holiday once you retire, or even every few years. But that is different to making holidaying your sole purpose, which will become expensive and very tiring after a while.

Short-term goals might be activities or purchases you want to achieve in the first five years of your retirement. They could be something as simple as renovating the kitchen or planting a new vegetable garden, but identifying them as short-term goals – especially in the case of holidays – separates them from your overall goals for retirement.

As with all goals, it is better to make them specific. Instead of 'Take an overseas holiday', try, 'Take a four-week holiday to France and Italy, including Paris, Nice, Bordeaux, Rome and Florence'.

Long-term goals

Your retirement could potentially last for three decades, so it's important you recognise this when setting long-term goals. These goals will include how you plan to achieve your passion or purpose and will also need to recognise your physical health at different stages of your life. It could be helpful to divide long-term goals into age brackets – for example, goals for ages 60 to 75, 75 to 80 and then 85-plus.

If education is your passion, then one of your long-term goals could be to get another degree in a subject that you purely enjoy rather than one that has a clear employment pathway. Another long-term goal could be to start and manage a farm. There is also nothing wrong with making spending more time with your children and grandchildren a long-term goal – maybe just put some boundaries in place.

Lifetime goals

What legacy do you want to leave behind? Do you want to leave something for your children and grandchildren? Perhaps you want to establish an endowment or foundation for a particular person. Would you like to be able to send somebody through university who wouldn't be able to afford tertiary education otherwise? Or would you just like to leave enough money for your children to be able to pay off their mortgages?

Many lifetime goals will need to be included in your estate planning, so don't forget to add them into your will and speak to your family about how you would like these goals implemented.

Your plans for aged care need to be considered as well. If you don't want to go into an aged care home, you need to work out what you do want to do instead and how you are going to fund that. The earlier in your retirement you can plan your aged care, the better, as many aged care advisers report that the older people get, the more reluctant they are to engage with this topic.

Nothing is too big or too small, and remember, there is no judgement. Spend a few hours writing down everything you want to do and achieve in your retirement, and then decide if they are short-term, long-term or lifetime goals.

Protecting your health, both mental and physical

If you want to have a long and fulfilling retirement, you need to consider your health. This doesn't mean you have to be in peak physical condition, but you need to understand the importance of physical activity throughout your lifetime and especially as you age.

The cost of not being physically active

According to the Australian Institute of Health and Welfare (AIHW), physical inactivity contributes to:

- 20 per cent of the total disease burden of type 2 diabetes
- 16 per cent of the total disease burden of coronary heart disease
- 16 per cent of the total disease burden of uterine cancer
- 12 per cent of the total disease burden of bowel cancer
- 12 per cent of the total disease burden of dementia
- 9.2 per cent of the total disease burden of strokes
- 3.2 per cent of the total disease burden of breast cancer
- 5.2 per cent of total deaths.

AIHW reports that an extra 15 minutes of brisk walking five days a week has the potential to reduce disease burden due to physical inactivity by an estimated 13 per cent. If you can double your weekly activity to an extra 30 minutes five days a week, the disease burden could be reduced by 26 per cent, with particular benefits for people aged 65 and over.

AIHW also says that people aged 65 and over should be doing at least 30 minutes of moderate-intensity physical activity on most days. These moderate fitness activities could include brisk walking, swimming, golfing with no cart, aerobics or water aerobics, cycling, yard and garden work, tennis, and mopping and vacuuming.

Strength activities are also important as you age. By keeping your muscles and bones strong, you will be able to do more physically for longer. Flexibility and balancing exercises are important for preventing falls. If you haven't already, include some physical activity as part of your goals.

Fortunately, being physically active has positive impacts for your mental health as well. It's important to recognise that retirement is a massive psychological change, with many people reporting an impact on their mental health. Beyond Blue says that simple things you can do to improve your mental health include:

· sleeping well
· keeping active
· eating well
· establishing a good routine
· practising mindfulness
· connecting with others
· getting help early if you feel your mental health is not good.

It might be a long road, but your retirement years could be some of the best years of your life. You will need to do a lot of planning for the financial, physical and emotional changes that you are about to experience. The more plans and goals you can put in place now, the better off you will be when you actually stop working.

Action points

1. Track down every superannuation and investment account you own. Don't forget to ask the Australian Taxation Office (ATO) if you have any lost super accounts.

2. Work out at least five short-term goals, at least five long-term goals and two or three lifetime goals for your retirement. For example, a short-term goal could be to spend two weeks in Paris in the summer, a long-term goal could be to become a member of a not-for-profit board and a lifetime goal could be to establish a foundation for neurodiverse kids.

3. Book in time with your partner to discuss, perhaps over a coffee or a glass of wine, when you would like to retire. If you are already retired, write down what stage you are in and what you have enjoyed most.

2

When to retire?

Compare the pair:

1. You are an experienced lawyer working for one of the top law firms in the country but heading ever so quickly towards retirement. Your employer has your retirement strategy planned out in advance, including when you will switch to part-time and, eventually, into forced retirement and ad hoc consulting.

2. You are a self-employed tradie working for yourself and have done little in the way of future planning. Your body is starting to give up on you after decades of building Australian homes, and you have made the decision to retire.

You could insert any number of alternative roles into these examples and the result would be similar: the decision about when to retire is vexed and complex. Yet it is one of the most important decisions of your life, whether it is forced upon you by your work, family or other commitments or determined of your own volition.

As lifetime financial advisers, we are in the privileged position of not only seeing this decision being made by hundreds of families every year but also being able to guide each family through this sometimes difficult journey. And this decision *is* a journey, and it involves your whole family, along with any number of additional stakeholders.

Through running retirement-focused events across Australia and hosting the popular *The Australian Investors Podcast*, we get the benefit of seeing first-hand people's successes and failures in retirement. If we have one message for you, it is that it is never too late to plan.

As much as you may believe your situation is unique, we can assure you it is not. We have seen every possible permutation multiple times.

When is a good time to retire?

If you're starting to think about transitioning into retirement and are keen to set an end date to the nine-to-five, cut back your hours or change the kind of work you do, then you are not alone. This is something that thousands of Australians grapple with every day. We know this because we've talked about it often on podcasts and held popular events for people considering when and how to retire.

The actual data shows that 140,000 Australians retire every year, or about 2700 every week. That seems like a lot, doesn't it? The average age of people who retired in 2020 was 64.3 years, according to the ABS, and at the time of writing about 673,000 workers plan to retire in the next five years. The average age of retirement is going up, although this is driven by women staying in the workforce longer; interestingly, it is decreasing for men. While anecdotal, it would seem to us that this is driven by the stronger financial position of men overall and, in general, the need for women to continue saving.

The decision to retire is a very individual choice with a broad range of drivers – some financial, some physical, some emotional and some circumstantial. According to the ABS, the top three reasons for ceasing work are:

· reaching retirement age or the eligible age to access superannuation (28 per cent)
· a health challenge, such as sickness, injury or disability (13 per cent)
· being retrenched or dismissed and unable or unwilling to get back into the workforce (7 per cent).

Looking at these statistics, people most commonly choose to retire once they can access their super and/or the government age pension, which is determined by when they were born (see Tables 2.1 and 2.2).

Table 2.1: when you can access the age pension

Birth date	Age when you can access the age pension
1 July 1952 to 31 December 1953	65 and 6 months
1 January 1954 to 30 June 1955	66
1 July 1955 to 31 December 1956	66 and 6 months
After 1 January 1957	67

Table 2.2: when you can access your super

Birth date	Age when you can access your super ('preservation age')
Before 1 July 1960	55
1 July 1960 to 30 June 1961	56
1 July 1961 to 30 June 1962	57
1 July 1962 to 30 June 1963	58
1 July 1963 to 30 June 1964	59
After 1 July 1964	60

Whether you choose to stick it out until the official pension age or leave the workforce early, the choice should always be yours. (Conversely, there is no legal requirement to stop working, either.) Let's look at the most common reasons for retirement aside from reaching age limits:

· **Health concerns.** As you age, generally speaking, your health declines – and then there is the infinite spectrum of health issues to which humans are prone. You may simply become unable to work, particularly if your job requires physical effort, as with the tradie in our introduction. Alternatively, your decision to retire might be prompted by your being in excellent health and being motivated to enjoy retirement while you are still fit and healthy.

· **Motivation/burnout.** You may be one of those people who loves their job and enjoys doing it. Alternatively, you may be someone for whom work has always just been what you do to earn a living. If you are part of this latter group and you're finding the thought of getting out of bed every morning and going to work increasingly harder to contemplate, it could be time to activate retirement plans.

- **'My work is done'.** It's a cliché but, as with all clichés, it is grounded in truth: towards the end of your career, it is natural to feel that there is no more you can achieve. If you are satisfied and can look back on your career fondly, you may get the feeling of having reached a natural end and that retirement is the next logical stage in your life. If so, then it is time to embrace it!

- **Family responsibilities.** With a fast-ageing population, you may be one of the many Australians dealing with parents who are coming toward the end of their lives. The desire to help could be an important factor in the mix of reasons for your retirement. Alternatively, you may simply want to spend more time with your children and grandchildren.

- **Forced retirement.** While forced retirement on the grounds of age is no longer legal in Australia, there are many other ways you can be 'forced' into retirement. Among the most common is a traditional redundancy, in which your position within a business is deemed to be no longer required and you receive a redundancy payout as a reward for your years of service. This is increasingly common among larger corporations and businesses operating in traditional sectors such as manufacturing, energy and mining. Less common is dismissal, which can be driven by misdemeanours at work. Even in a booming job market, if you have spent a loyal career in a single sector, you may find it difficult to retrain and find work in the new economy.

· **Selling a business.** For many small business owners or partners, retirement means stepping down from running your business. The ABS estimates that more than 100,000 baby boomers in Australia will be looking to sell their businesses between 2023 and 2026. You may have to negotiate 'golden handcuff' or 'earnout' agreements, which represent restrictions on your ability to sell a business and walk away. Many small business owners do not have much in the way of super when the time comes to retire, likely meaning the business is their 'super', which only increases the importance of a clean exit.

For most people, the decision of when to retire will come down to the question of whether they have enough money (see Chapter 3). In many ways, answering this financial aspect of retirement is simple, but it is the emotional side that is much more challenging.

For singles with sufficient assets, the decision may well be straightforward, but for those in a relationship the decision is more complex. One of you may wish to retire earlier than the other. If so, the partner who decides to retire early may set up their own life and hobbies only for their partner to 'disrupt' this or seek to join in.

Irrespective of the age when you retire, what's important is to plan for a longer retirement than you expect. This is in part because research shows we're now living longer than ever, and disease cures and management are improving. Factoring in improvements in life expectancies over the last 25 years, half of today's 65-year-olds will live to at least 87 if male and at least 89 if female. A healthy couple entering retirement can expect one or both of them to live for 30 more years.

Of course, not everyone will stop working on Friday and be retired on Monday. Many will semi-retire, cut down their hours or switch their type of work to something more manageable. And, of course, there is 'pretirement', the period of time before you retire when you prepare yourself mentally and financially and begin to plan for the next phase of your life (see Chapter 1).

Semi-retirement

Semi-retirement is an increasingly popular concept: more and more retirees no longer abandon the workforce entirely when they retire but instead choose to continue working in some capacity. The impact of the rising cost of living will likely have an ongoing say in this decision too.

The reasons may be financial, or they may simply be inspired by the wish to stay active or to keep contributing at a lower level of exertion. You may be involved in a family business or a farm, or you may find that your expertise and experience is valued by younger colleagues or family members. You may also be looking forward to trying something different – for example, volunteering at a charity.

Whatever the motivation, working during retirement has become increasingly common, and the trend shows no sign of abating. The grey area of partial involvement can be a fulfilling way to ease into retirement.

Unretirement

Amid the stream of Australians retiring, there is actually a flow going the other way. Plenty of individuals are deciding to 'unretire', often for financial reasons but also, in many cases, because of boredom in retirement or a desire to do something different than in their careers.

As much as 40 per cent of the nearly half a million people who entered the labour force over the three years to October 2022 were over the age of 55. Nationally, almost one in five of all workers, or 19.6 per cent, are now aged over 55, up from just 11.4 per cent two decades ago.

This trend was well under way even before record-high inflation and cost-of-living pressures emerged over 2022 and 2023, a set of circumstances that is placing pressure on many households to make ends meet – retirees included.

Transitioning to retirement

In 2005, the Australian Government introduced the Transition to Retirement (TTR) provisions, which had multifaceted aims but which effectively endorsed the ability for individuals to transition to retirement by reducing their work hours or shifting to a less demanding role in the later years of their careers. Before the introduction of TTR in 2005, workers aged under 65 had to cease employment fully before accessing any superannuation benefits. In 2004, the government noted that this may have led to 'people deciding to retire prematurely just so they can access their superannuation'; at the same time, the government had realised that many older people wanted to keep working, and that there were economic and social benefits to the country if that were encouraged.

The emotional aspects of retirement

Retirement can be a hugely emotional event. Whereas you used to get up in the morning, go to a workplace and do your job, earn a salary and be known and valued for what you did, in retirement that all disappears. On the other hand, you suddenly go from being quite fixed in your day-to-day activities to having freedom and flexibility. For many, this is a dream come true and you revel in the change, but others find the change hard to handle.

Retirement is unknown territory, no matter how many family members and friends you've seen pass through the portal.

Retirement coach (and former super fund chief investment officer) Jon Glass has seen it all in retirement. He has seen people struggle to find worth and meaning in their lives, missing not only their purpose and the structure of their working week but suffering from 'relevance deprivation' and an unravelling of the identity that work gave them.

One question that Jon says took him by surprise came from a client who asked, 'Will I still be an interesting person when I'm retired?' That implies quite heavily that this person's identity is very connected with their job and retirement is a disconcerting thought for them.

Jon recommends that people approaching retirement think as hard about developing a diversified portfolio of personal pursuits as they do about diversifying their investment portfolio. This helps them establish a new sense of identity and boosts self-worth because it allows retirees to describe themselves according to what they do – for example, writer, house husband, surfer or cyclist.

'Another key aspect of retiring is recognising that your work, your contribution, your colleagues, have provided you with a sense of self-esteem and self-worth for decades,' he says. 'You have to fill in those gaps.'

Jon says it's natural that people ask, 'Will I be bored?' He points out the flip side, which is, 'How are you going to take full advantage of all this time you're going to have?' Your retirement could last for 10,000 days. As we've noted, remarkable increases in life expectancy mean retirees can expect to live as long as another 30 years after finishing work. Medical research says engaged lifestyles can improve health, bolster cognitive capacity, delay physical and mental decline and boost longevity.

Courtesy of the advertising industry, we tend to picture retirement as grey-haired couples looking at a sunset over a beach while having a drink. But that's not retirement; that's a holiday. According to Jon:

> 'There's a traditional approach to retirement that's known as the "three Gs": golf, gardening and grandparenting. And that approach works for some people but not for everyone, because you can do those things, but you can be more adventurous as well, and that's what a retirement coach can do – open your eyes to more adventurous possibilities. Keeping active and engaged has clear health benefits; the benefit from increased social connections and engagement is incalculable.'

It is all about being as prepared emotionally as you are financially. First, this means that you and your spouse or partner don't have different retirement plans and are on the same page, because retirement can affect relationships. Second, it means that you are psychologically prepared to find new sources of purpose and fulfillment in retirement.

Do you have enough interests and hobbies?

Planning memorable, pleasurable and life-altering experiences is a fun thing to do, but it is even more fun to experience them. The best part of retirement is setting a whole new schedule and having the freedom to explore and pursue your passions and hobbies. After spending the majority of your life at work, you might not know what to do with all of this new free time.

Hobbies and interests are essential for a fulfilling and satisfying retirement experience. Engaging in hobbies and pursuing your interests can give you a sense of purpose that easily matches – and hopefully exceeds – that which your working life provided.

A great way to prepare for retirement is to challenge yourself to think outside the box in terms of things you want to do and achieve. Then, trying to tick-off your golden list – some call it a 'bucket list' – is a great way to keep your focus on extending and challenging yourself, thinking about your life in creative and constructive ways, and not falling into contemplating the passing time.

It is common for couples to start retirement with a bang, travelling to Europe, seeing the sights and doing all those things they missed out on while at work. Next comes a renovation, or perhaps helping the children buy their own homes. But once these things have been checked off, what comes next? This is where the bucket list needs to move beyond travel and towards experiences. Have you always wanted to build your own wooden furniture, learn to play bridge or even skateboard? Whatever it is, the world is your oyster.

Where to call home?

Where you are going to live in retirement is another huge question for retirees and can be a significant cause of anguish.

The concept of 'downsizing' or even 'upsizing' is one of the first decisions that many will face. If you are a home owner, there are sound reasons for selling the family home and moving into a smaller dwelling. Selling your home and downsizing can free up money for paying off your mortgage, investing or spending. A smaller home comes with less upkeep responsibility, lower insurance and cheaper utility bills. By downsizing, you'll have less responsibility, a smaller workload, increased cash flow and greater flexibility, all of which help reduce stress. You can choose a layout and fittings that better suit your needs, or a location closer to family, transport and services. Also, you can access the benefits of making a downsizing contribution into your superannuation, which we discuss in Chapter 6.

Another way to monetise the value of your family home is to exchange some of its equity for cash that you can then use to fund your retirement. There are a few ways you can do this:

· A **reverse mortgage** uses the equity in your home as security to provide you with a loan. The loan only needs to be paid off (plus interest and fees) when you sell the house or die, whichever occurs first.

· In a **home reversion or equity release arrangement**, you sell off part of your home equity – in other words, you sell off a share of the future value of the home – in exchange for a discounted lump sum amount, or instalment payments. However, you can continue living in your home. Your share of the equity in your home reduces over time to cover the fees you pay.

· The **Home Equity Access Scheme** (HEAS) lets eligible older Australians access the equity in their home (or other Australian real estate) through an Australian Government loan. The scheme allows a person to access fortnightly loan payments to 'top up' any pension payment they receive to a maximum of 150 per cent of the maximum fortnightly rate of age pension (including the pension and energy supplements, and rent assistance, where applicable).

As always, make sure you take professional advice before you take any of these steps.

Moving into retirement accommodation

Where you live in retirement may change over the years, and one day you might consider moving into retirement accommodation.

There are two types of people when it comes to retirement living. Some vow never to leave their own home, ever! Others see a pathway from downsizing to moving into purpose-built accommodation, with a high-care facility in close proximity. If you're open to this, there is plenty to think about when making this decision.

Retirement accommodation ranges all the way from 'over 55s' villages that look like luxury resorts – and appear to be full of healthy-looking younger retirees living an easy-living, active lifestyle – to high-care retirement villages that are definitely more 'aged care' than 'retirement living'. But there are plenty of excellent options in between.

There is a wide array of arrangements and service offerings (for example, strata title, loan and license, leasehold and rental agreement) and fee structures (for example, entry, ongoing and exit fees) that need plenty of research and good advice. Among the best sources of information are myagedcare.gov.au and nationalseniors.com.au.

Shift to aged care

The change from retirement accommodation to aged care is another of the big decisions facing retirees. While some see the shift as linear, it is anything but. You may be one of those people who remains mobile into their old age and thus more likely to utilise the growing range of in-home support packages, both public and private, to retain your independence, or you may be all but forced into 'aged care' due to a lack of support or worsening health.

An aged care home (sometimes known as a 'nursing home' or 'residential aged care facility') is for older people who can no longer live at home or in their retirement accommodation and need ongoing help with everyday tasks or healthcare.

Leaving where you currently live and entering an aged care home is not an easy decision, but it doesn't have to be a daunting or sad experience. An aged care home can give you the care and services you need to maintain your quality of life. The government funds a range of aged care homes across Australia so they can provide care and support services to those who need it. Each aged care home is different, so it's important to choose the right one for you; again, do your research and seek good advice.

The majority of readers will be years off considering aged care living, though, so let's look next at how much is enough (financially) to fund the retirement lifestyle you will be happy with.

Final action points

1. Write down five things you would like to have done over the last 12 months but couldn't due to your work commitments.
2. Ask yourself, *If I knew I had enough money to retire today, what would I do? Would I keep working? Change jobs? Quit tomorrow?*
3. Contact your employer and ask them about flexible or part-time working arrangements should you wish to transition into retirement.
4. BONUS: don't be afraid to explore ideas about where you will live in retirement – in both the early and later stages.

3

How much is enough?

The question of how much is enough is the most difficult to answer, both in finance and in life. Like many of life's most vexed questions, the real answer is, 'It depends'. Understanding how much money you might need in retirement depends on a range of factors, and as much as we wish there were a simple number for everyone, it just isn't the case.

Your retirement number will be determined by both measurable and immeasurable outcomes, such as:

- how many assets you begin retirement with
- how your investments perform during retirement
- how much you spend in various phases of retirement
- when you spend this money
- any additional government benefits you may receive
- how long you live and how healthy you remain.

Naturally, the outcomes are incredibly diverse. To illustrate this, let's compare two retired couples who have had very different experiences during their golden years.

Kerry and Sam began retirement with significant wealth of around $1.5 million in superannuation in addition to both their home and a beach house, which they owned outright. Once they both stopped going to work and began spending more time in their home, it became obvious that a renovation was required. Rather than seek a loan, which can be difficult for those over 60, they chose to fund the renovation through their superannuation balance knowing that they would one day need to sell their home or their beach house to continue funding their lifestyle. The challenge was to deal with the emotional impact of seeing their capital decline month after month as living expenses were paid from a dwindling balance.

On the other hand, Pat and Kim retired with a reasonable super balance of $800,000 and a home without any debt. They live a 'comfortable lifestyle', drawing around $48,000 per year (about 6 per cent of their balance) from their fund, and they have drawn this amount every year for 15 years. They also benefit by being eligible for the Commonwealth Seniors Health Card, which keeps some prescription and other health costs low (see Chapter 8). The investment returns achieved by their financial adviser have been above average for a balanced portfolio but, interestingly, they have managed to maintain the same balance for close to a decade. They are ecstatic; while their capital hasn't grown, it has not been reduced, and for those in drawdown phase this is a significant win.

In this chapter, we combine the data-driven perspective of funding your retirement with the emotional and qualitative overlay that makes these decisions more challenging in the real world.

The numbers

The problem with most things concerning finances is that they rely on averages, and most people are anything but average.

For instance, Table 3.1 shows the average superannuation balance for certain demographics.

Table 3.1: average superannuation balances
for certain demographics

	Men	Women
Aged 55 to 59	$316,457	$236,530
Aged 60 to 64	$402,838	$318,203

SOURCE: AMP REPORT, 2023

Do these averages sound like you? Does this feel like enough?

While the Australian retirement system is seen as one of the most progressive and successful in the world, super fund members' confidence in retirement remains incredibly low, due to lower levels of financial literacy and perhaps engagement due to the default or forced nature of the system.

The Association of Superannuation Funds of Australia (ASFA) stands out as the premier source of information on retirement. Its 'retirement standard' suggests that you need income of more than $31,000 a year in retirement for singles and more than $45,000 a year for couples to fund the expenses of a 'modest' lifestyle. If you want a 'comfortable' lifestyle, which ASFA defines as enabling 'an older, healthy retiree to be involved in a broad range of leisure and recreational activities, and to have a good standard of living through the purchase of such things', a single person would require income of $50,207 a year and a couple would require $70,806 a year. Assuming annual investment earnings of 6 per cent, a couple would need $690,000 in retirement savings to fund the 'comfortable' lifestyle (through a mix of their own savings and the age pension), while a single person would need $595,000 – a long way from the average super balances noted in Table 3.1.

Planning your spending

Whatever amount you start retirement with, your situation will be determined by debit and credit: how much you spend versus how you add to your balance, whether through work or investment returns.

How much will I spend in retirement?

According to the Australian Government's Moneysmart website, the rule of thumb is that you can expect to spend about 67 per cent of your current income annually in retirement.

There are three very broad phases you will experience in retirement:

1. The **active phase** is when you typically enjoy full health and want to maximise your lifestyle options through travel and leisure activities – think caravans and overseas flights.

2. The **passive phase** is when, as you get older, your activities become less intense. You travel and go out less – think domestic trips and more time with family.

3. The **frail phase** is when health concerns (and costs) tend to dominate and your spending is focused on maintaining your health as well as possible and supporting your basic living needs, as opposed to discretionary or lifestyle expenses.

However, like all of the other major parameters of retirement, spending behaviours are highly individual.

Capital versus non-discretionary expenses

Obviously, everyone has needs, and these are covered by your non-discretionary spending. Much of this does not change with retirement, and includes essential groceries and living expenses, shelter, electricity and other utilities, essential clothing and shoes, healthcare, insurance, taxes, rates and interest on any debt.

Then there are your discretionary or capital expenses, which are not strictly essential; these are the things you like to have. This includes travel (and the associated insurance), golf club and gym memberships, streaming TV subscriptions, electrical goods, dining out, spending on your hobbies and interests, donations to charities, and helping children and grandchildren – for example, contributing to private school fees for the latter.

We call these 'capital' expenses as they contribute to greater enjoyment in your life, or 'investing in yourself'. We know that people derive happiness from buying 'experiences', such as trips and sharing special meals and wine with family and friends, and that they will try to keep doing these things for as long as they can.

You might have your own list of spending priorities that aren't strictly 'essential' but you consider necessary to allow you to continue to be who you are. There are no wrong answers in this regard.

Other factors that eventually come into play are the level of care you require versus what you have budgeted for, whether you own your own home and whether you want to leave your children any money.

Importantly, the level of age pension and Centrelink support an individual receives can be a game changer in providing a safety net.

The curveball of getting older

Thanks to better nutrition, awareness about bad habits, improved medical knowledge and technology, we are living longer than ever before. Australian women have added 25 additional years to their average life expectancy in a century; one in two women will reach the age of 85. As we mentioned earlier, average life expectancies are expected to continue to rise, reaching 87.0 years for men and 89.5 years for women by 2063. Of course, these numbers are only predictions based on expected averages. In reality, there is a wide distribution of actual lifespans either side of the average.

On the face of it, the fact that we are living longer than ever before is good news. However, for most of us, that positive thought is tempered by the conundrum of 'longevity risk' – can you afford to live that long while maintaining the lifestyle to which you have become accustomed?

With the cost of living rising sharply over 2022 and 2023, longevity risk has become an increasingly prominent issue. The 2023 National Seniors Social Survey of almost 6000 people aged 50 and over found that 53 per cent of older Australians believe they will outlive their savings. Solely cutting spending is not a sustainable long-term strategy for older Australians to manage rising costs of living as most expenses fall into the 'essentials' camp, while discretionary expenses tend to be closely tied to the enjoyment of one's life.

Again, every individual's situation is different, but with compulsory super being such a relatively young policy, average retirement balances are nowhere near where they need to be, and so a big challenge for you will be to plan for retirement income that will last a lifetime.

How to structure your income in retirement

The financial and investment world is prone to both over-complicating simple matters and oversimplifying complex matters. Nowhere is this more apparent than in the retirement space, in which concepts such as determining your risk level based on your age or always drawing the same per cent of capital every year are seen as foolproof or 'guaranteed' plans.

Retirement is not a linear process, and it resists being easily modelled. However, some broad approaches are worth highlighting.

The 4 per cent rule

The 4 per cent rule suggests that you can safely withdraw 4 per cent of your savings each year in retirement for at least 30 years.

This 'rule', is really more of a generalisation; it is not meant to work for everyone. The 4 per cent rule was roughly premised on the common 60:40 asset allocation: 60 per cent shares and 40 per cent bonds. This asset allocation tended to help investors because shares and bonds were negatively correlated: when one performed poorly, the other made gains, buttressing the portfolio. It was never intended for one number to represent the experience of so many different individual retirees, but the media ran with the term and made it a famous 'rule'.

The Down Under version – the 5 per cent rule

At our retirement advisory firm, Wattle Partners, we have come up with our own rule of thumb. Our experience has shown that a broadly diversified balanced portfolio, with share allocations evenly split between global and domestic, should be expected to provide an income yield of 5 per cent a year in retirement.

A key part of this is the higher yields of Australian shares, driven by the history of franking credits, but also franking credits themselves. Australia's tax system is unique in that franked dividends are taxed less harshly than capital gains, which is the opposite of that which occurs overseas. The result is that, over many years, Australian companies have tended to focus on paying higher dividends to attract more investors and thus ensure their share prices remain supported. This means that if you rely solely on overseas shares, you will be forced to draw into capital regularly given the lower yield from most investments.

This rule of thumb is intended to give you confidence that the income will come over the long-term, and thus you need to focus on living your life rather than focusing on every dollar deposited into your bank account.

Filling your buckets

Another common approach to saving for retirement involves setting up 'money buckets' that split your savings into three sources:

1. The **short-term** bucket holds six months of your living expenses and income requirements in cash and highly liquid term deposits. It is your main, immediate financial buffer.
2. The **medium-term** bucket contains three years' worth of living expenses and income requirements in high-quality, low-to-medium-risk assets such as government bonds, credit, property, infrastructure and some blue-chip shares.
3. The **long-term** bucket is dominated by stocks and other growth assets, such as real estate investments. This part of the portfolio is likely to deliver the best long-term capital growth, but the returns in this bucket will vary more than the other two buckets.

The buckets are refilled by interest income, dividends and other gains from your investments. At some point each year, the buckets need to be rebalanced. Our experience has shown this should occur once a year at the very least, but the optimal rebalancing period is every quarter in order to gain the benefit of dollar cost averaging (explained in the glossary at the back of this book).

The logic of the bucket strategy is that regardless of the short-term performance of the long-term bucket, pension payments can continue from the other pools without you having to sell down the growth assets at potentially unfavourable prices. As your short-term cash needs are covered, you won't have to worry about the fluctuations in the stock market.

Going nowhere is winning

One of the biggest misconceptions we see in the thousands of people we meet is the expectation that their super balance will continue to grow every year and that they should leave it intact for their family. The reality is, the entire system is actually set up to do the exact opposite: you are forced by legislation to draw more money out of super as you age. This doesn't, however, mean you need to spend it.

While you have spent your entire life seeing your capital increase, at some point it will do the opposite, and this will be uncomfortable. As a result, holding ground may well be winning at times.

Forms of retirement income

Australia's retirement income system has three pillars: the age pension, compulsory super and voluntary savings, which includes voluntary superannuation contributions, housing and other assets. Most older Australians will rely on all three pillars for income during their retirement.

The mix is different for everyone, and some of the elements affect others. For example, your account-based pension forms part of the income and assets test that affects your eligibility for the age pension. For others, the age pension is important, acting as a guaranteed income stream, protecting you from inflation and investment risk.

The age pension

The age pension is a key pillar of Australia's retirement income system. For most people, some form of government pension will be an important part of their individual retirement income mix.

Your eligibility for the age pension depends on several factors, including a means test of your assets and income. Almost 70 per cent of Australians over age pension age received some form of Australian Government pension or other income support payment in 2022–23.

Super account-based pensions

An account-based pension (or 'allocated pension') allows you to draw a regular income stream from your super, meaning you don't have to take your super as a lump sum. Your money stays invested and will benefit from a tax-exempt status.

You can choose the size and frequency of your payments within the minimum or maximum allowed. You can also make extra withdrawals when needed – for example, if you want to have a holiday or renovate your home.

You also get to choose how much you want to transfer to the 'pension phase', subject to the transfer balance cap (which currently sits at $1.9 million and is indexed to inflation). Payments continue until the account balance runs out or you take what's left as a lump sum. How long your account-based pension lasts depends on:

- the amount of super you transfer to your pension account
- how much you take in payments each year
- super investment earnings (which are tax-free)
- how much you pay in fees.

Your personal savings and assets

Personal savings and assets such as property, shares and managed funds, held outside super, can also make up part of your income in retirement. How you manage your assets is based on many factors, such as what they are, what they are worth and when you need to free up the cash invested in them.

Home equity

Given that well over 80 per cent of people over the age of 65 own their home outright, home equity should almost be considered the fourth pillar of retirement income. There are various ways to access it, some of which we covered in Chapter 2.

The inheritance dilemma

One issue we tend to ignore rather than forget is that most of us will receive an inheritance, and this should also be factored into planning.

Receiving a sizeable inheritance can certainly change your retirement plans, but planning on an inheritance can be risky. Many variables can affect the size and timing of your inheritance, and most of these are out of your control. Consider making an independent retirement plan and using your inheritance as a supplement.

For many, an inheritance is a blessing and provides unexpected improvements to lifestyle and the value of your estate, but sometimes it can impact your age pension entitlement, in which case it may not be a blessing.

The undrawn super dilemma

A paradox is emerging in Australian retirement: retirees aren't spending, even when they can afford to do so.

Superannuation was never intended to enable large balances to be built up – on the back of generous taxpayer assistance – that are then bequeathed to the next generation. An individual's super is meant to fund their own retirement. The government wants retirees to spend not only their investment earnings but also their capital amount.

The obvious rejoinder to this from retirees is, 'It's our money, and we'll do what we want with it'.

A 2022 survey of more than 3000 retirees conducted by National Seniors and annuity provider Challenger reported the alarming news that almost one in four retirees (23 per cent) have no intention of drawing down their superannuation and about half want to preserve at least some of their capital, and virtually none are tapping into their housing equity.

The reasons for the reluctance to spend are varied, but they are mostly psychological: about 84 per cent of people who want to retain some of their super cited concerns about medical and aged care costs. People are too uncertain about the future.

Action points

1. Put pen to paper and write a list of all your assets and liabilities. Put everything into a Microsoft Excel spreadsheet, then split it into 'lifestyle' and investments assets.

2. Put 30 minutes aside to think about 'your number' and write it down. That is, try to work out the amount of money you need in your bank account, just in cash, to sleep well at night.

3. Download ASIC's household budget from the Moneysmart website and put aside two hours to track your expenses from the last six months.

4

Build your team of experts

Pat and Peter Jones are both 55 and heading towards retirement. They are medical specialists – Peter is a paediatrician and Pat is a general practitioner – and have never taken a great interest in financial matters aside from the basics, preferring to extend their knowledge in areas that could ultimately help their patients. Like most families, they have focused on educating their three children, paying off the mortgage and investing in property, giving little thought to retirement.

As their sixties drew closer, they realised they needed some professional help with their finances. They knew what they wanted to do in retirement – travel overseas every couple of years, downsize out of the five-bedroom family home, and enjoy their hobbies of golf and horseriding – but they were not sure if they were in the best financial position to do this. They also wanted to retire early – before 62, if possible.

Pat is earning around $200,000 a year and Peter around $300,000. They have two separate superannuation accounts of $700,000 and $600,000, and own their home and the property that

Peter's paediatric clinic operates from. They have just $50,000 in savings combined.

Pat and Peter could pool their superannuation and start a self-managed superannuation fund (SMSF). They could also make a downsizer contribution from the proceeds of the family home of up to $300,000 each. They could also potentially move Peter's clinic property into their SMSF as it qualifies as a business real property. The SMSF would then allow them to accumulate capital in a very low-tax environment and build a passive income stream.

These are quite complex strategies, and so it would be best for a financial adviser to outline them in a financial plan and for Pat and Peter to build a team of experts to help facilitate and implement the plan. But having such a plan in place gives pre-retirees like Pat and Peter confidence in their ability to achieve their goals. This confidence is key, as once people realise they have enough money to retire, they often feel increasing joy in their lives and work and are happy enough to maintain part-time employment for several years.

In addition to a financial adviser, the Joneses' team of experts would need to include a property adviser or agent to help with the sale of the properties, a solicitor for legal advice around the business real property and an accountant to help with tax planning. Also, their SMSF needs an auditor once it is established.

The costs of such an expert financial team are not insignificant, but by helping implement these proposed strategies they could help the Joneses enjoy a retirement income of close to $200,000 for the next 30 years.

The role of financial literacy

The *Cambridge Business English Dictionary* describes financial literacy as 'the ability to understand basic principles of business and finance'. While a financial adviser is an expert in this field, we all need to be financially literate enough to manage our daily finances and understand and interpret financial advice, if we decide to seek it.

Not knowing how to manage your money can be disastrous, with consequences ranging from simply not getting the returns that you should through to falling victim to fraud. As scammers become increasingly sophisticated, it's even more important to maintain a good level of financial literacy so you avoid becoming one of the hundreds of Australians who lose money to scammers each year. Australians lost $3.1 billion to scams in 2022 alone.

Overall, Australians are relatively financial literate, and we get more knowledgeable as we get older, according to the Australian Government's National Financial Capability Survey 2021. That survey found our average financial literacy score was 68 (out of 100), increasing to 74 for those aged between 55 and 64 and 76 for those over age 65. More good news is that most people over 55 years old also have a financial plan for retirement.

The value of financial advice

If you were able to ask the Joneses for the value of the advice described at the beginning of this chapter, they might say it was invaluable, because what a financial adviser was able to give them dramatically changed their retirement outlook and was something they could never achieve on their own.

A good financial adviser will take the time to get to know you and understand your individual needs. They understand that doing so will put them in the best position to help you set and achieve appropriate financial goals. Just as you would hire an architect to create a plan for your home, you employ a financial adviser to create a plan for your finances and investments. Their advice can cover a wide range of areas, including budgeting, investing, superannuation, retirement planning, estate planning, insurance, tax and technical strategies.

A financial adviser is an expert in the world of finance, investment and superannuation, a world that can seem quite complex to people who don't operate in it daily. A good financial adviser will be most valuable on the technical side, helping you get better investment returns than you could otherwise have achieved and pointing out tax strategies that you were unaware of.

Just as important as putting you in a better financial position, having a financial planner can also make you happier. Research from financial services industry research firm CoreData conducted on behalf of Fidelity demonstrates that a good financial planner adds not only money but happiness to people's lives. That report found that 88.5 per cent of Australians receiving financial advice believe it has given them greater peace of mind financially, and 86.2 per cent believe it has given them greater control over their financial situation.

Basically, people who have an adviser and a financial plan in place are much more likely to understand and be in control of their future than people who don't. And those two things are very strongly aligned to happiness.

Achieving financial goals

Just like your individual circumstances, your financial goals are many and varied and will differ depending on your age and life stage. Figure 4.1 shows the top three financial goals of 404 people surveyed by CoreData were having appropriate investments, having a savings plan and getting the most out of their superannuation.

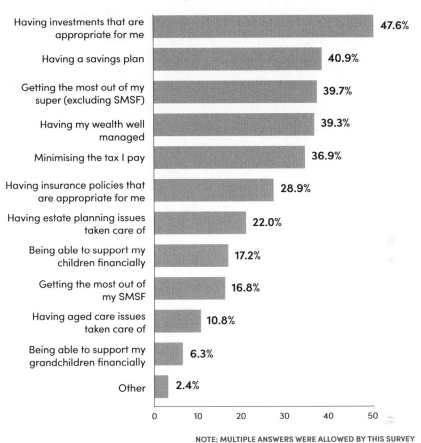

Figure 4.1: what financial goals has receiving financial advice helped you achieve?

NOTE: MULTIPLE ANSWERS WERE ALLOWED BY THIS SURVEY

Financial needs generally become more complex as you approach retirement, so this is when engaging a financial adviser is crucial in helping you achieve your retirement objectives.

Your personal retirement goal could be as simple as enjoying a similar standard of living to what you have today. However, unless you are a financial professional, you are probably not aware of the many strategies available to you that could help you achieve this goal. For example, did you know about the downsizer contribution that we mentioned was available to the Joneses at the beginning of this chapter? We will go into this strategy in more detail in Chapter 6, but if you are aged over 55 and looking to downsize a family home, this one strategy alone could provide a vital boost to your retirement funds.

This unique knowledge and understanding of how many different financial strategies apply in different circumstances are financial advisers' bread and butter and are essential for helping people attain their financial goals.

Security and confidence

When it comes to investing, many financial professionals colloquially refer to the 'sleep at night' test. This is a measure of how much risk people are willing to take in their investments. There is no point, for example, in investing in a high-growth investment fund, which also comes with a higher risk of capital loss, if it keeps you awake at night worrying.

A financial adviser can help you understand your risk profile and what investments you will be comfortable with and why. They can then suggest investments that will fit that risk profile. Remember, a good financial planner will never pressure you into investing in something; what they should do is give you the confidence to understand the investments that are most appropriate for your circumstances.

The financial system is significantly more complicated than many people appreciate. More importantly, the unfortunate prevalence of poor investments and outright scams has increased the need and value of both a sounding board and an expert opinion.

As mentioned earlier, money lost in financial scams has more than tripled in recent years to over $3 billion. ASIC, the investment regulator, also wages a constant battle against innocent-sounding but misleading or deceptive advertising by investment promoters. The value of working with a trusted financial adviser really can be priceless.

The cost of advice

Good advice costs money. Financial advisers guide people through a complex and sometimes quite confusing financial and investment world, and just like any professional that provides a valuable service, they should be appropriately rewarded for the expertise, service and outcomes they provide.

Fee facts

How and what financial advisers charge has been a vexed question for some time as regulators, industry bodies, investor organisations and governments have argued over transparency and consistency. In 2019 the Australian Government finally ended the payment of product commissions from fund managers, which had been the mainstay of most advisers' remuneration for many years. However, financial advisers are still allowed to charge commissions on insurance products.

There are several different types of fees that your adviser could charge, including the following:

· An upfront fee
· A set annual fee based on the type of client and the services provided
· A percentage of the funds under management (FUM) or funds under advice (FUA)
· An hourly rate.

Whatever fee combination is used, the adviser must always charge what is fair and reasonable. This is a requirement under the *Financial Planners and Advisers Code of Ethics*. The adviser must be able to explain and defend the charges, agree the amounts with the client in advance, and document them in the Statement of Advice (SoA) to ensure there are no surprises for clients. If they are advising on financial products, which is often the case, they need to outline the fees they receive from this in a Financial Services Guide (FSG) as well.

According to Adviser Ratings' *Australian Financial Advice Landscape Report 2023*, the average cost of financial advice rose by 40 per cent in five years to $4250 in 2022, with expectations that would rise further in 2023 on the back of CPI increases. That fee may seem steep at first glance, but it covers the cost of an in-depth SoA that details a series of sophisticated financial strategies designed to optimise your wealth and your retirement income. Also, consider the return you're getting on that initial outlay. The Joneses profiled earlier have been able to access thousands of dollars of retirement income they wouldn't have been able to receive otherwise.

What price should you expect to pay for a comprehensive document that outlines your entire life on a page, compared to what we pay unthinkingly to sell our house or buy a car? In the context of being able to sleep easily because your investments and retirement are well planned, is $5000 really expensive? Naturally, we all look at the cost, but the value of good advice goes well beyond that initial payment in every aspect.

Robo-advice

As the cost of providing advice for advisers has increased, the type of clients they are willing to deal with has leaned towards those with significant amounts of financial wealth. However, because of recent improvements in financial technology, opportunities to serve clients with lower balances have emerged. These types of services are called 'robo-advice' or 'digital advice', and they can automate many of the processes involved in managing investments. They use online questionnaires to assess investors' risk profiles, goals and investment timeframes, which make their services low-cost compared to a full-service adviser.

Most robo-advisers use exchange-traded funds (ETFs) to build portfolios that can be diversified across various asset classes and geographical regions. However, they rarely provide technical advice. Robo-advisers are opening up the world of investment to people with much smaller investment amounts.

What to be wary of in a financial adviser

Just as there are qualities to seek out when you are considering a financial planner, there are also several red flags that should prompt you to at least ask more questions, if not leave the room.

Fee red flags

One of the biggest red flags is evasiveness or a lack of clarity regarding the fees being charged. The adviser should have no problem explaining how they are charging.

Be wary of a financial adviser who charges a percentage-based fee. It does not inherently cost more to manage $10 million than $1 million. The adviser's fees should be based on the service provided plus the risk element with an acceptable profit margin.

Also, never, ever pay money into an adviser's personal account.

Advice red flags

At minimum, your adviser should hold an Australian Financial Services (AFS) licence, or be an authorised representative, employee or director of an AFS licensee or an employee or director of a related body corporate of an AFS licensee. You can find a list of registered advisers at moneysmart.gov.au/financial-advice/financial-advisers-register. Your adviser also needs to be authorised to provide personal advice in relation to 'relevant financial products' to retail clients.

If you have concerns, you can also check the banned registry at asic.gov.au/online-services/search-asic-s-registers/banned-and-disqualified.

A financial adviser who is product-driven rather than relationship-driven is another red flag. An investment product should be an outcome of advice, not the driving factor behind it. Question excessive enthusiasm for a specific fund.

Investment red flags

ASIC considers a 'wholesale client' or 'sophisticated investor' someone who can certify that they earn $250,000 a year or have more than $2.5 million in net assets, including the family home. A 'sophisticated' or 'wholesale' investor can access investment opportunities that 'retail' investors cannot, but in doing so they also lose some rights – chief among them the requirement to have fees disclosed. A financial adviser who wants to classify you as a wholesale investor when you clearly do not have the assets or income is not to be trusted.

Always be hesitant of advice from a financial services product manufacturer or institution that also controls your capital. These kinds of organisations may try and upsell various other products they provide. Also, just because a fund or an investment has performed well in the past doesn't mean it will continue to do so, so ask questions if an adviser is suggesting an investment based on its historical performance.

Size and resource red flags

A financial advisory shouldn't be so small that their advisers are run off their feet, and neither should it be so big that you get lost among the masses. You should be able to see that the business has the appropriate governance and support levels. It needs to have the appropriate financial planning software and team members who can help with back-office functions. A one-person show in a shopping centre or shared office space is a red flag.

Adviser checklist

Take this list with you when you visit a financial adviser, and always remember to seek a second or third opinion if you don't feel comfortable. Also, before you even attend the first meeting, check if they are registered at moneysmart.gov.au/financial-advice/financial-advisers-register. Ask yourself:

- Is there real rapport?
- Does the adviser listen to and address everyone in the meeting – that is, both spouses in a couple?
- Does the adviser ask questions about your personal and financial goals?
- Does the adviser ask questions about your attitude to risk?
- Do you understand the adviser's explanations – that is, they don't use complex language or jargon?
- Is the advice the adviser suggests clear?

- Is the advice appropriately diversified across a range of investments?
- Is the information the adviser gives you about fees easy to understand?
- Does the adviser answer all your questions?
- Does the adviser have at least five years' experience?
- Does the adviser or their firm have appropriate resources to do their job properly – that is, they are not a one-person show?

Building your expert team

Investing and finance is a complicated area, and the reality is that there will not be one person with the expertise and knowledge in all the areas you could potentially need.

Finding a good financial planner is your first step but should not be your last. That person simply will not have the solution to every problem you may encounter. The best advisers recognise the role of experts in their field and will assist you to build a competent team of financial professionals and life experts to help you with what's most important.

Tax adviser

There is a stark difference between a tax adviser and your run-of-the-mill accountant. Both may have studied accounting at some point, but the tax adviser will be vastly more experienced in a range of tax strategies that may be useful for your retirement planning. And once you've entered retirement, it's not all plain sailing when it comes to tax, and the potential for expensive mistakes is still there. It may not be wise to assume that doing it yourself, or always referring to your family accountant, will cut costs.

A simple example of such a mistake is when people make contributions that are tax deductible but they don't have any income to deduct those contributions against. That can have the unintended consequence of triggering contributions caps, which can end up being quite costly.

If you decide to establish an SMSF, you will also need a tax adviser or tax accountant who specialises in SMSFs, especially once you enter retirement and start paying yourself a pension from your SMSF.

Other specialised situations in which tax advisers really come into their own include selling a business, bringing offshore assets back to Australia or understanding executive staff plan shares. A tax adviser's expertise in these areas could save you thousands of dollars. The last thing you want is to get an audit from the tax office four or five years into your retirement querying a claim you made as a small business owner that results in you having to pay thousands of dollars back to the ATO.

Estate planning specialist solicitor

The estate planning essentials of will preparation and administration, and appointing powers of attorney, are key components of any retirement strategy. A power of attorney can make financial and legal decisions on your behalf if you lose the capacity to do so, and it is important to appoint them while you have legal capacity. Having a sound legal will in place will make sure your assets will be divided among your dependants as you wish.

When somebody dies without a will, or 'intestate', state and territory laws determine how the estate will be inherited. In some states and territories this can exclude foster children, stepchildren and in-laws. It will also delay the distribution of your estate, with the matter potentially tied up in courts for a long period of time.

A good estate-planning specialist solicitor will make sure they understand your wishes and put a will in place that ensures those wishes are enacted and your assets are appropriately protected. The estate plan should then be reviewed every two to three years or if your circumstances change.

Your financial adviser can also play a role in helping your solicitor understand familial relationships. This is another reason why it's important to have a team. These different financial professionals are most likely to find the best financial outcome for you when they collaborate.

There are other areas of the investment process where a solicitor's advice may be needed, especially when it comes to some SMSF investments, such as real property. The Joneses would have needed a solicitor, for example, when transferring ownership of their business real property to their SMSF.

We discuss estate planning further in the next chapter.

Property adviser

Selling a property, which often happens when people downsize close to or during retirement, is usually one of the biggest financial decisions that anybody makes. It can also be fraught with emotion, especially if people need to sell properties they have lived in for years or raised families in.

A property advocate or adviser acts on your behalf and deals with real estate agents. They play an important role by removing the emotion from the equation. They can help simplify the process of buying and selling property, and they have unique knowledge of the industry, which means they are in a good position to find the best prices. They usually charge a percentage of the agent's fee.

Their advice isn't limited to downsizing, either. Some new retirees may actually be planning to spend more time at home and may instead choose to upsize. In these cases, a good property advocate will know where their dollar might go further.

Retirement coach

Retirement isn't just about finances, although that is of course very important. While a lot of emphasis is put on being financially prepared for retirement, there is not much support for the psychological side of retirement. The mental health impacts of retiring are real, especially for people who have had much of their self-worth tied up in their work. Although the idea of never working again can seem attractive in the build-up to finishing work, some people can find the actuality of retirement a letdown.

A specialist area within the growing field of life coaching that can help with this is retirement coaching. Retirement coaches help retired people with the life changes, both physical and mental, that come with the onset of retirement. Through a number of one-on-one sessions, they can help the newly retired, or about to be retired, find meaning in their new life and provide them with some purposeful goals to work towards.

A personal trainer

If you want to live a long and happy retirement, then you need to prioritise your health. Doing some form of moderate exercise, such as brisk walking, for just 30 minutes a day is known to reduce the risk of heart disease and stroke, increase muscle and bone strength and improve balance.

Engaging a personal trainer is a very good way to make sure you stay in shape and keep to those exercise goals. This is not about breaking any sporting records; it is merely about maintaining a healthy lifestyle. A professional can keep you accountable and, most importantly, understand your health needs and requirements.

Friends and community

Exercise isn't the only thing that can extend your life; having an active social life and a strong friendship circle has also been shown to improve longevity. And, unfortunately, the reverse – social isolation – is known to increase your chances of developing dementia.

So, if you truly want to enjoy a long, healthy and happy retirement, make sure you work at making and keeping friends throughout your life. This will involve time and effort, but the mental payoff in your twilight years will be worth it.

Action points

1. Book a meeting with your financial adviser and accountant, and ask for an update on your situation. If you don't have either, start interviewing two or three to at the very least review your situation.
2. Consult the household budget you made after reading the previous chapter and highlight those expenses you no longer think will be relevant once you retire.
3. Add a tab to your household budget and list every fee or cost that you are being charged on your finances, along with the services you are receiving.
4. BONUS: Ask your adviser or accountant if you are being treated as a 'wholesale' or 'sophisticated' investor.

5

Future-proofing and estate planning

It's a staple scene in Hollywood movies: a person's last will and testament is read out in front of the family, friends and (always) people whom no-one else present knows. Someone is elated, someone is disappointed, and someone plots vengeance, as the testator laughs from beyond the grave.

In the real world, the estate-planning process can be even more dramatic than the finest Hollywood movie. As divorce, separation and blended families become increasingly common, the complexity and importance of estate planning only continues to grow.

Consider, for instance, David and Margaret: a twice-married couple both with children from prior marriages. Each family has accumulated varying levels of wealth throughout their own lives but with very different backgrounds and relationships with money and their family.

With only a portion of David and Margaret's assets accumulated while they were together and held in varying levels of ownership, including an investment property, a principal residence, an SMSF and a small commercial property, there is a significant amount of complexity. This complexity is exacerbated by the differing financial and health situations of each potential beneficiary. Too often this sort of complex situation is put into the 'too hard' basket, and ultimately left to the courts to resolve. The problem with this, of course, is that it is prone to legal challenges, in which case the only real winners are the law firms involved, with their fees paid by the estate. With Australia set to embark on the largest intergenerational wealth transfer in history, having a valid will has never been more important.

Wills

A will is simply a written document that sets out what you want to happen to your property and assets – your estate – after you die. Once the will maker has died, the executor (or executors) submits the will to the appropriate court with the support of a solicitor.

The executor is responsible for making sure all of your assets are accounted for, debts are paid and all beneficiaries receive their inheritance as directed in the will. One often-overlooked issue when creating a will is when people name an executor of a similar age to them, who naturally may be unable to perform their duties when called upon.

Once the court grants probate (recognition that the will is valid), the distribution process can begin. Your executor must deal with the will within 12 months from the will maker's date of death.

Every person should have a will!

Creating a will is one of the most important things you can do for yourself and your family. Unfortunately, it is too often put to the side or seen as an unnecessary cost.

Most Australians still don't have a will. In November 2022, financial services comparison site Finder released a nationally representative survey showing that 60 per cent of Australians – equivalent to 12 million people – do not have a will. That finding was despite a 33 per cent rise during the pandemic of people making a will. Less than one in three Australian women (31 per cent) have their affairs in order, compared to half of men (50 per cent).

If you are over 18, you can make a will – as long as you have the mental capacity to understand what you are doing, which is an increasing issue for our ageing population and the prevalence of dementia.

The witnesses of your will must be independent, in that they are not beneficiaries of the will who could influence you when signing, and they must understand the general nature of your will, which is to facilitate the transfer of assets upon your death.

If you die intestate – that is, without a will in place – the court gets to decide where your assets go. This is the worst-case scenario. For instance, if you are separated but not divorced, your estranged spouse would have an entitlement to your estate.

Interestingly, in Australia, courts have a dispensing power that allows them to admit a will to probate as long as it is a document – which includes phone texts and audio recordings – and the court is satisfied that you intended the document to operate as your will.

When there is no relative or other person entitled to claim on your estate, it's likely the estate will pass to the state or territory government under succession law. If your children are under 18, the funds will be managed by the Public Trustee.

A will may be found invalid if it was fraudulently created or if the will maker was influenced to draft the document in a particular way, such as through pressure from a family member. It is not a good idea to run the risk of the court finding your will invalid.

Even if your family gets a favourable outcome through the courts, it will hold up the probate process and require court time, which is expensive and time-consuming.

DIY wills

As is the case with most professional services, you get what you pay for.

For those who are unable or unwilling to bear the cost, there is always the option of doing a simple 'do-it-yourself' (DIY) will through a template easily available online from a range of government agencies, newsagents and bookshops. A DIY will kit can certainly help you to create a convenient and affordable legal will that allows you to clearly appoint an executor (or executors) and set out how you wish your estate to be divided after your death. However, it not be able to handle even slightly complex situations such as blended families or SMSFs, let alone afford your beneficiaries flexibility and valuable tax advantages, which can extend into the thousands of dollars.

Estate lawyers love DIY wills because they are so good for the will-challenging business.

Who gets what?

There are no hard and fast rules about what must go into your will, but it surprises many people that some assets are automatically included in your estate and some are not.

Your estate includes any property you own at the time of death, including:

- assets, such as houses, cars, money, shares and investment properties

- rights and powers, such as the right to appoint the trustee of a family trust
- specific belongings, such as jewellery, books, artworks, pieces of furniture and musical instruments.

Among the most confronting parts of losing a loved one is the transactional manner in which most institutions will treat you. Bank and other accounts will be closed off immediately. This is where it is key to understand whether you own assets with your partner jointly or as 'tenants in common'. Assets owned as joint tenants will be immediately transferred to the other owner (you). For assets held as tenants in common, however, each 'share' of the asset is an asset in and of itself and thus could form part of your will separate to your partner, and could be passed to someone other than your partner.

Similarly, there are many assets that aren't automatically captured in your will. Chief among them is your super account, but this also applies to a number of structures generally used to manage tax liabilities or grow businesses, such as family trusts and their underlying assets.

The fact that super is a 'non-estate' asset is surprising to most people. Who your super balance can be paid to is restricted both by the law and by the behest of the trustee of your super fund, which may be the super fund itself or, if you run an SMSF, your spouse.

You can direct your super to your estate via a death benefit nomination, in which case it will be treated the same as every other asset. It can be incredibly difficult have your assets paid efficiently from your industry super fund, but the binding death benefit nomination remains the most foolproof option.

Family trusts are further removed than superannuation, with most trusts having an initial lifespan of 80 years, meaning they can last several generations. While the control of a family trust can pass via the will, the underlying assets will not, with this being one of the biggest benefits of the structure – that is, the ability to skirt potential death taxes in the future.

Paying out super

The payment of your super balance on death is determined by:

- the existence of a binding death benefit nomination
- the discretion of the fund's trustee
- the rules of the superannuation fund.

Only superannuation dependants of a person can receive their super payment directly. They could be:

- a spouse (which includes a de facto partner)
- a child (regardless of age)
- a person who was financially dependent on the deceased at the time of their death
- a person who was in an interdependent relationship with the deceased at the time of their death.

Changing a will

Life changes quickly. It's important to review your will regularly so that it keeps up with changes in your life.

The simplest way to change a will is to make another one. Making a new will automatically cancels the old will and takes the place of any will that you had before.

You should always make a new will if you:

- get married
- have children

- divorce or separate
- buy a significant asset or investment
- invest in a new business, company or trust.

You can revoke a will by physically destroying the document, such as by burning, shredding or recycling it.

You can also change a will by adding a codicil to it. A codicil is a legal document that allows you to make changes to your will without having to create an entirely new will, potentially keeping the out-of-pocket cost low.

De facto relationships and wills

De facto relationships, in which two people are not married but live together or have lived together as a couple on a genuine domestic basis, are increasingly common. Unmarried spouses in a de facto relationship are treated the same as married spouses. The same laws apply to same-sex couples as heterosexual couples.

When one spouse passes away without leaving a will, the other spouse inherits. When a child or other claimant contests a distribution to an unmarried partner, the issue typically revolves around whether or not there was a de facto relationship.

Protecting your will

The real reason that you should have a will in place is to minimise the risk of challenges to your estate and final wishes. A valid will all but removes contention and, when possible, the risk of your assets being used to fund legal fees for aggrieved beneficiaries far and wide.

Your will can be challenged by any eligible person who believes it is unfair to them. An 'eligible person' is any person who could reasonably have expected to be included in the will or treated better by it. This generally includes:

- a spouse or domestic partner (this includes same-sex partners) at the time of your death
- a child or stepchild
- a person who for a substantial period during your life was treated as a child or dependant.

More wills are being challenged nowadays, almost solely due to the increasing number of divorces. One in three marriages will end in divorce, with the average marriage lasting 12 years. This means that blended families are becoming increasingly common. The greater prevalence of blended families means that more people may feel they should be recognised in a will.

Here are some other reasons driving challenges:

- **Greed.** The property boom means that even a modest family home in a capital city may be so valuable to so many people that it is worth fighting for a slice of the sale proceeds.
- **Longevity.** Australians are living longer, which means there is more time to build up considerable assets.
- **Ageing.** As people are dying later, their children's lives upon receiving inheritance have become radically different: someone dying at about the age of 90 can have children who are in their fifties, sixties or even seventies.

Testamentary trusts

Among the most misunderstood parts of any estate plan is the role and value of a 'testamentary trust'.

Put simply, testamentary trusts are established in wills to own and protect some or all of your assets. A testamentary trust is created by your will to take effect upon your death. It distributes your estate to various trusts established by your will, rather than transferring the assets to individual beneficiaries directly. Thus, there are clear asset-protection benefits for complex family situations. The testamentary trust holds the entitlement on behalf of your nominated beneficiaries, and the trustee has discretion to decide which of your beneficiaries receives income and capital distributions each financial year.

The true benefit of testamentary trusts is the tax-planning opportunities they offer. Children under the age of 18 can receive income through a testamentary trust and be taxed at the normal adult marginal tax rates, not the punitive minor rates.

Testamentary trusts are also able to offer some protection of family assets, and are often called 'bloodline trusts'. Because the assets held by a testamentary trust are not owned by the beneficiaries, they are not available to the creditors, spouse or partner of the beneficiaries following the breakdown of a marriage or de facto relationship.

Say a son divorces his wife several years after his parent's death. If the parent, when making a will, leaves the son's share of the estate to him directly, then the ex-daughter-in-law could seek a share. However, if the son's intended share of the estate was instead left to a family trust that he and his siblings controlled, he would not legally own that share of the estate – and so his ex-wife would not be able to seek a share of the trust assets.

Also, if you think that there is any possibility that a beneficiary might spend or dispose of their inheritance irresponsibly, a testamentary trust is a powerful vehicle because the trustee holds the assets on behalf of the beneficiaries and can limit access to both income and capital.

Powers of attorney

Much of this chapter has been dedicated to the impacts of an estate-planning strategy after your death, but Australia's ageing demographic means we must consider estate planning before the grave. While incredibly sad, the prevalence of dementia and Alzheimer's disease (and similar diseases) is leaving a growing cohort of Australians unable to make decisions for themselves from a much younger age than expected.

For instance, Phillip suffers from Parkinson's disease and has, over years, lost the cognitive ability to make any real health or financial decisions. Without a power of attorney, Phillip will rely on either the courts or the benevolence of his family members, many of whom are spread across the world, for the support he needs.

Unfortunately, not all of us have the support we anticipate at the times in our life when we truly need it. This makes the 'power of attorney' an important part of any estate plan.

A power of attorney is a legal document that allows you to choose who will conduct your financial, legal or personal affairs if you are not able to make these decisions yourself. Like a will itself, setting up a power of attorney can be a difficult step for you to take: we simply do not like envisaging ourselves in a situation where we do not have the capacity to make decisions for ourselves.

In any case, a power of attorney can be implemented if you are undergoing an operation, going overseas for an extended period or will be any other situation in which decisions may need to be made when you are not present. A power of attorney can be thought of as an additional level of insurance.

All people aged 70 or older should have appropriate powers of attorney in place, and younger people may need to have them in place depending on their individual circumstances.

There are three types of powers of attorney, and each power is different and suited to different situations:

- A **general non-enduring power of attorney** allows you to authorise a person to act on your behalf in relation to your financial matters.
- A **supportive power of attorney** allows you to appoint a person (or up to four people) you trust to help you make your own decisions while you have capacity to make decisions.
- An **enduring power of attorney** means that your attorney can make financial and personal decisions on your behalf if you are unable to do so due to injury or illness. You can choose for the enduring power of attorney to start straight away or only when you have lost capacity. The enduring power of attorney lasts until either you revoke it or the end of your life.

Medical decisions

Everyone wants to make their own medical treatment decisions, but it's always possible you could experience an injury or illness that means you are unable to make these decisions. Some states and territories allow you to appoint a person called your 'medical treatment decision maker', who has legal authority to make medical treatment decisions for you.

You can also state the medical treatment you would like to have in future by making an 'advance care directive'. Your doctors and your medical treatment decision maker have to follow this directive in most cases.

Action points

1. Track down the original copies of your wills and powers of attorney, if you have them. If you don't, contact a solicitor or financial adviser as a matter of urgency.

2. On a single page, write down who you wish to receive each of your assets, including anyone who you think may need some sort of additional support.

3. Contact your superannuation fund, or accountant for SMSF owners, and ask for a copy of your binding death benefit nominations.

6

Tax and super do the heavy lifting

Former nurse Joan Stone is 66 years old. She is a single parent but her two children left home a decade ago, and she is waiting on the birth of her first grandchild. Due to a productive working life and some savvy financial decisions made early, along with salary sacrificing into superannuation for most of her career, she is now ready to retire with $600,000 in superannuation.

Joan is quite keen to take a pension, but she also wants to leave some funds aside for a world trip in a year's time and plans to upgrade her car in the next five years. She thinks $100,000 should cover those costs, and she hopes that $500,000 will be enough to fund her retirement and it won't run out before she does (metaphorically speaking).

To start her pension, she shifts $500,000 into an allocated pension product with her existing industry superannuation fund and leaves the remaining $100,000 in her accumulation fund. However, she notices that the investment options available in the pension product are quite limited. While her industry fund has served her well until now and she previously did not have the time to consider an SMSF, she is wondering if the benefit of being able to decide where her funds are invested might make an SMSF worth it.

Also, Joan doesn't realise that while the earnings on the $500,000 in her pension account will be tax free, the earnings on her accumulation fund will not be. This means that if the $100,000 manages to return 8 per cent – or $8000 – while she is waiting to use it, she would have a tax bill of $1200 that she could have avoided.

Joan's situation is a good example of how important it is to understand all the ins and outs of superannuation and how its tax effectiveness can best suit your individual needs. Once you hit retirement, superannuation becomes a lot more complex, and you may need some help to work out the best strategies.

Even before you hit your late fifties and start seriously planning your retirement, it's a good idea to have a basic understanding of how to make superannuation work for you across your life.

What is super?

In a nutshell, superannuation is a tax-effective savings vehicle for retirement. Since July 1991, employers have been required to make superannuation contributions for their employees. This contribution, called the superannuation guarantee (SG), started at 3 per cent in 1991 and is set to rise to 12 per cent by July 2025 (see Table 6.1).

Because the Australian super system is still relatively young, policy settings and product developments to date have largely focused on the accumulation phase. The industry is only just starting to look at more effective structures and products for fund members who have moved into the retirement phase to draw down their money.

The challenge of retirement is that you have a finite pool of capital to protect and live on. Understandably, this can create some concern and anxiety. However, while the retirement phase of life requires a different approach to the career phase, this can be managed very successfully and is not something to be afraid of.

Table 6.1: superannuation guarantee percentage

Period	Percentage
1 July 2002 to 30 June 2013	9
1 July 2013 to 30 June 2014	9.25
1 July 2014 to 30 June 2021	9.5
1 July 2021 to 30 June 2022	10
1 July 2022 to 30 June 2023	10.5
1 July 2023 to 30 June 2024	11
1 July 2024 to 30 June 2025	11.5

The tax benefits of superannuation

Superannuation is a tax-effective savings vehicle because it is taxed differently than your regular income. Contributions paid into your superannuation fund by your employer are taxed at 15 per cent, as are additional contributions from your before-tax salary up to a certain limit, which are also called salary sacrifices or concessional contributions.

Your superannuation fund's investment earnings are taxed at 15 per cent while in accumulation phase. If you're aged 60 or over, all your income from an account-based pension or annuity, including investment income, will be tax free.

However, there are some limits on the tax treatment of superannuation and pensions, introduced because the government was concerned it was too attractive and was thus being used as a tax haven by some millionaires. There is now a limit on how much you can transfer from accumulation phase to pension phase to fund a retirement income; this is the transfer balance cap, which, as noted earlier, currently sits at $1.9 million and is indexed to inflation. Also, from 1 July 2025 earnings corresponding to an individual's balance above $3 million will be taxed at an additional 15 per cent.

What are the different types of super funds?

Superannuation does not have to be difficult to understand, although it is easy to see why many Australians might think it is complicated. As stated earlier, it is basically a savings vehicle with some special tax advantages designed to relieve pressure on the social security system. There are a number of different types of superannuation funds, but they all serve the same purpose and operate under the same superannuation laws.

At the time of writing, Australians have a total $3.5 trillion invested in superannuation in the five main types of funds: retail funds, industry funds, public-sector funds, corporate funds and self-managed superannuation funds (SMSFs):

- **Retail super funds** are typically run by a bank, an investment company or some other financial institution and generally aims to make a profit, some of which may be paid in dividends to shareholders. They are public-offer funds and open to anybody.

- **Industry super funds** are 'profit-for-member' funds and began life as superannuation vehicles for workers in defined industries; for example, the Health Employees Superannuation Trust Australia (now HESTA Super Fund) was for people employed in health industries. Most of the industry funds are also now public-offer funds as well.
- **Corporate super funds** are also profit-for-member funds and are offered to employees in a particular company. The corporate-fund sector is shrinking, but large employers such as Telstra and Qantas still offer such funds.
- **Public-sector (or government) super funds** are run by governments for employees in the public service and government agencies. They're also profit-for-member funds.
- **SMSFs** are small funds that are set up and managed by individuals. They can have up to six members who are in total control of the investment process.

Your 'stapled account' (see Chapter 8) follows you as you change jobs, but you can choose to change it whenever you like, and portability of super makes this easy. You can also consolidate superannuation benefits into one account to reduce fees and charges.

Big numbers

Australia's total superannuation assets amount to $3.5 trillion. The median annual growth fund return since 1992 is 7.8 per cent.

Retail super funds

Retail superannuation funds are open to anyone and are generally run by banks or investment companies. Unlike industry funds, profits go back to the company's owners not members.

Historically, retail funds held the lion's share of the Australian super kitty, but since 2019 the industry funds have moved well ahead. At the time of writing, retail funds hold $680 billion, or 19.5 per cent, of all super – half of what they held 20 years ago. Retail funds delivered a five-year annualised rate of return of 4.5 per cent to June 2023, according to APRA's performance data.

Most retail funds offer a wide array of investment options for members to choose from, and these may even include options to invest directly in shares. They may have higher investment fees than industry funds as a result. Some new products that have entered the market recently, such as Vanguard Super, offer very competitive price points.

Industry super funds

Industry superannuation funds were originally set up to serve workers within a specific industry. They were first established in the 1980s to offer an alternative to the high-fee and commission-bearing products that were then common in the retail superannuation market.

With a total of $1.16 trillion in assets under management at the time of writing, industry super funds account for the largest chunk of total superannuation assets at 33 per cent. The largest industry fund, AustralianSuper, holds about $290 billion on behalf of more than 3.1 million members. The second-largest fund, Australian Retirement Trust, manages more than $240 billion on behalf of 2.2 million members.

As of June 2023, industry funds delivered a five-year annualised rate of return of 5.8 per cent according to APRA's performance data.

These profit-for-member funds offer members a wide range of investment options catering to different risk appetites. These range from defensive, with higher allocations to 'safer' assets such as cash or bonds, right through to high growth, which have much higher allocations to listed equities. Many also now offer different kinds of ethical or socially responsible investment options for people who don't want their assets invested in industries such as coal and tobacco.

As with all large funds, they are now required to offer a default MySuper product, which usually has lower fees and simpler products and will be the option your employer pays your super into if you don't make an active choice.

What is MySuper?

In 2013, the Australian Government introduced a simple, cost-effective super product called 'MySuper'. MySuper products are not allowed to charge entry fees, hidden fees or commissions to financial advisers. MySuper replaced existing default funds, but only those funds with a default product that met the MySuper standards were able to operate as a default fund. MySuper products hold just over a quarter of total Australian superannuation assets.

In August 2021, APRA conducted its first annual performance test for large superannuation funds. The test looks at administration fees over the past financial year and investment performance over an eight-year period, and was designed to help members compare MySuper options. If a MySuper product is rated as 'underperforming' for two consecutive years, it has to advise members that they're in an underperforming fund, and it can no longer accept new members until it is rated as 'performing'.

Self-managed superannuation funds (SMSFs)

There are a lot of attractions to running an SMSF. It gives you a greater ability to tailor your portfolio to suit your needs, it enables you to invest directly and when you retire it pays you a pension. It also gives you more control over how you design your eventual retirement benefits, and you can optimise tax and estate planning strategies.

Like all superannuation funds, the investment income and capital gains of your fund are taxed at only 15 per cent. You can reduce this rate even further by using the imputation credits on franked dividends (dividends on which the company has already paid tax) to lessen or even eliminate the fund's tax liability on its earnings and the tax on contributions, and also by using the discounted rate of capital gains tax (CGT) for assets held for more than 12 months. Then, when your fund moves to paying you a pension, it pays no tax on earnings or capital gains, and it receives rebates for the franking credits that it no longer needs to use.

If you are considering an SMSF, you will have a number of legal responsibilities and there are penalties for breaching these. First, an SMSF must have a trust deed, and all members must be individual trustees or directors of the corporate trustee. If you are not eligible to be a trustee or director, you cannot be a member of an SMSF. (You can check your eligibility at ato.gov.au by searching for 'Appoint your trustees and directors'.) Trustees must also 'formulate and implement' an investment strategy for the fund. All new trustees of SMSFs are required by the ATO to sign a trustee declaration formally acknowledging that they understand their duties, obligations and responsibilities.

An SMSF is also required to have a set of audited accounts prepared each year, and the trustees must lodge a tax return for the fund. Typically, that will mean your accountant will prepare the accounts and then arrange for the fund to be audited by a registered SMSF auditor. The accountant that prepares the returns cannot also do the audit.

Sometimes people fall into the trap of thinking that they can buy a beach house for their SMSF or a nice piece of art to hang on their wall. Buying either of these assets is perfectly legal, but very strict conditions on their use will apply; they must be used only by people at 'arm's length' to you, which excludes you, your relatives and friends.

Most SMSF trustees utilise a variety of specialist service providers to help them meet their obligations, and the expert team outlined in Chapter 4 is especially relevant for anyone with an SMSF.

Your super and myGov

You can manage your super using ATO online services through the myGov app if you have a myGov account. This enables you to:

- view details of all your super accounts, including lost or unclaimed amounts
- see your remaining concessional and non-concessional cap amounts
- view and use the personalised version of the YourSuper comparison tool
- consolidate eligible multiple accounts (including any ATO-held super) into one account
- withdraw your ATO-held super if you have met certain conditions of release.

How to boost your super

The superannuation guarantee will provide the basis of your retirement savings, but there are other ways to boost your superannuation over the course of your working life. At different life stages, different strategies will be more effective.

Strategies for thirties and under

While you are young is the best time to start making regular additional voluntary contributions to your superannuation, no matter how small. The magic of compound interest means that you earn interest on interest, which grows the longer the savings are here.

You can ask your employer to pay part of your pre-tax salary into your super account – either a percentage or a set dollar amount. This is known as a 'salary sacrificing' and can be part of a salary packaging arrangement. The payments are also called 'concessional contributions' because they are taxed at the super rate of 15 per cent. For most people, this will be lower than their marginal tax rate. You benefit because you pay less tax while you boost your retirement savings. If you set the amount of your salary to be sacrificed into super as a percentage, it will grow as your salary grows while you move through your working life.

There is a limit to how much extra you can contribute. The combined total of your employer and salary-sacrificed contributions must not be more than $27,500 per financial year. However, if you don't use all of this cap in a financial year, you can 'catch up' by making larger concessional contributions in a later year. Unused cap amounts can be carried forward for up to five years before they expire. To be eligible to make catch-up concessional contributions, your total super balance must be less than $500,000 at the end of the prior financial year. You can find out your unused cap amount by checking ATO services via myGov.

Joan (from the beginning of this chapter) began salary sacrificing when she was 25, and it made a significant contribution – an average of $10,000 a year over 41 years – to her $600,000 superannuation balance when she retired and was one of the defining factors in her being able to retire early.

Strategies for forties and over

It's not too late to start salary sacrificing into your super if you are in your forties. The impact of small amounts won't be as great, but your disposable income is probably larger than what it was in your twenties, and you may be able to sacrifice a larger percentage of your salary.

You can also make voluntary super contributions from your after-tax pay: these payments are called 'non-concessional' contributions, because you have already paid tax on the money. You can make non-concessional contributions up to $110,000 each financial year if your total superannuation balance (TSB) is less than $1.9 million.

Sometimes, with the costs of mortgages and children's education fees hitting hard, your forties can also be a period of stagnation when it comes to your retirement savings, and that is okay too. Just make sure you take advantage of the opportunities when they do come your way.

If you have recently received a large amount of money, such as an inheritance, you may also be able to take advantage of the bring-forward rule, which enables you to package up three years of non-concessional contributions caps, or $330,000, into one year. You need to have a TSB of less than $1.68 million on 30 June of the previous financial year to be able to use the bring-forward rule. The income earned on the inheritance in super would only be taxed at 15 per cent rather than your marginal tax rate.

You may also be able to make spouse contributions if your partner is earning a low income or taking time off work for caring responsibilities. You can do this by making a spouse contribution to their super account or arranging for contribution splitting (also known as super splitting). Spouse superannuation contributions can now be made for spouses earning up to $40,000 per year. If your spouse has earnings below $37,000, you can claim the maximum tax offset of $540 when you contribute $3000 to their super.

Strategies for those 55 years old and over

All the previously mentioned strategies for younger age groups are of course still relevant to people over 55 years old, but there is one particularly attractive strategy that is now available to people over 55 years old that can really help boost their superannuation balances later in life.

We have touched on this in previous chapters, but the downsizer contribution allows anybody over age 55 to contribute up to $300,000 of the proceeds of the sale of their home into their superannuation. It is available to each spouse in a couple if you are selling the family home together, which means a couple could make a combined contribution of $600,000 into the family SMSF. A downsizer contribution is a non-concessional contribution, but it does not count towards the contributions cap and only impacts your total superannuation balance when it is recalculated at the end of the financial year.

The home needs to have been owned by you or your spouse for 10 years or more, and it needs to be a home in Australia and not a caravan, houseboat or other mobile home. You won't get the same tax advantages from selling your investment property as you would your primary dwelling, but if you have some investment properties then this is a good time to put them on the market and contribute what you can to your superannuation fund. If the property is owned by your super fund and you expect it has experienced a decent capital gain since you bought it, you may be able to include that gain in your lifetime super CGT cap (1.705 million in 2023–24).

Similarly, if you have small business assets and are over 55, you may also be eligible for the small business 15-year exemption on the sale of a business asset that you have continuously owned for 15 years or more. You will then be able to reduce or disregard CGT on the sale and contribute the proceeds to superannuation if they are under the lifetime super CGT cap.

Finally, if you are in this age group you might want to start thinking about a recontribution strategy to reduce the tax component for the next generation. This involves withdrawing a lump sum from your superannuation and then recontributing it back as a non-concessional contribution, which has already had tax paid on it. When you pass away, your dependant will not have to pay tax on the now-larger non-taxable component in your superannuation.

How to access your super

Although you may be able to access your superannuation early in extenuating circumstances, most Australians will need to meet a condition of release to receive their superannuation. These include turning 65 (even if you haven't retired), reaching 'preservation age' (see Table 2.2 in Chapter 2), retiring or starting a transition-to-retirement pension while working.

A transition-to-retirement pension is an income stream you can receive from your superannuation, even if you're receiving an income from an employer or business. It is designed for people considering moving from full-time to part-time work as they transition to retirement. You can't cash out the super benefit because you're still working, but you can supplement your employment income with super income of between 4 to 10 per cent of your super balance each financial year.

You can also access your super if you're aged between 60 and 64 and stop working, even if you subsequently get another job with another employer. This is the case even if you have no intention of retiring completely.

You can access your superannuation as a lump sum or an income stream in the form of an account-based pension. While the Australian Government would probably prefer that most people turn their super into a regular income stream, what you do depends entirely on your circumstances; just make sure you are using the most tax effective structure that you can. If you decide to take a lump sum, it should be as simple as filling out a super retirement drawdown form from your super fund, which will also ask for a declaration that you have met a condition of release. The funds will then be moved into your nominated bank account.

Taking a pension

The major tool for taking an income from your superannuation once you retire is the account-based or 'allocated' pension, which offers a regular, flexible and tax-effective income stream. You need to meet the same conditions of release for an allocated pension as a lump sum withdrawal. There is now a limit, called the transfer balance cap, on how much you can transfer from accumulation phase into pension phase, which is currently $1.9 million.

If you are starting an allocated pension with an existing industry or retail superannuation fund, there will usually be an application form on their website to fill out. This will typically ask how much you want to transfer to the 'pension phase' (subject to the balance transfer cap), the size and frequency of your payments (see Table 6.2 for minimum drawdown rates; if you are drawing a 'transition to retirement' pension, the maximum drawdown rate is always 10 per cent of your 1 July balance) and how you want your super invested through your fund.

Table 6.2: minimum pension drawdown rates

Age	Rate
Under 65	4.00%
65 to 74	5.00%
75 to 79	6.00%
80 to 84	7.00%
85 to 89	9.00%
90 to 94	11.00%
95 or over	14.00%

If you have an SMSF, starting a pension is a little more complicated. You need to value the assets within the superannuation account that will be supporting the pension. If you still have members in accumulation stage, you may also need to segregate the assets or get an actuary to proportion which assets are in each stage and provide an actuarial certificate. You also need to draw up a pension agreement, which details the frequency and value of payments, the pension start date, documents such as an annual pension statement that needs to be produced once a year, and how variations can be made to the pension. A product disclosure statement also needs to be supplied, which includes the main details and features of the pension.

There may be more involved in setting up an allocated pension from an SMSF, but as Joan discovered at the beginning of this chapter, you can have much more input into the investment strategy of an SMSF pension than you would in a mainstream fund, and that can be especially attractive to people who are interested in investment and have a bit more time on their hands in retirement.

The other major retirement income product is the annuity, also known as a lifetime or fixed-term pension, which gives you a guaranteed income for a certain number of years or the rest of your life. Individuals can use their super (or savings outside of super) to buy an annuity from a super fund or life insurance company if they have reached their preservation age. An annuity is less flexible than an account-based pension, but you can be sure about your future income.

Super and insurance

Superannuation funds are required by law to offer basic levels of life and total and permanent disability (TPD) insurance to members of MySuper products. The sheer size of some of the larger super funds means that they can negotiate competitive group contracts for value cover that likely would not be available to members through individual policies.

For new super fund members aged under 25 or with account balances lower than $6000, insurance is only provided if those members request it. Some funds also offer income protection insurance.

SMSFs are also required to have at least considered members' need for insurance.

Action points

1. Login to myGov, or register at my.gov.au/en/create-account if you haven't already, and check your total superannuation balance.

2. If you have a retail or industry super fund, check your member statements and find out the taxable or tax-free components and whether you are in accumulation or pension phase.

3. Download as much information as you can about your super fund and see if it is right for you. Do you know where your money is invested? Does this align with your values? How has it performed? Would you like more control?

7

Retirement-focused investment strategies

Let's step back to 2020 and the middle of the pandemic. Arguably the most impactful event in modern history had seen the global economy mothballed and, as a result, disruption and volatility spread throughout financial markets like wildfire. Share markets experienced the most significant falls and eventual recovery in decades, while bond markets all but froze amid the volatility.

Investors and retirees were caught between being worried for their health and worried about their finances. During periods of immense stress, it is natural that we seek to control anything we can, and this includes our finances and investments.

Consider Daniel and Georgia, for instance, who had vastly different responses to the volatility. Georgia was more comfortable with risk than Daniel and saw the significant market falls in March 2020 as a time to hold course and wait for the market to recover. Daniel, on the other hand, was a little more conservative, and after seeing the market drop as much as 20 per cent in just a few days he felt the need to take action. In his view, his only option was to 'protect' what capital he had left by switching his super fund to a more conservative option.

While few expected the market to recover as quickly as it did, history has shown that capitulating during periods of market stress is the most damaging action anyone can take. The result was that Daniel locked in significant losses in his super fund and did not benefit from the eventual recovery.

This case study offers a unique insight into why investing in retirement is truly different to every other part of your life: primarily, because every single dollar is difficult to replace and thus precious. This illustrates the need for a 'framework' from which important decisions can be made.

Much of the investment industry suggests that investing in retirement is no different to investing during other periods of your life. This, in our view, is wrong.

Investing in retirement requires a complete shift in the thinking and approach that guides investment decisions. Once you turn on the 'retirement' switch, you are now limited to a finite pool of capital that needs to last as long as possible to fund your retirement.

The key in this stage of your life is to invest for resilience, for multiple outcomes and, most importantly, to minimise the number and severity of financial mistakes.

The retirement challenge

The challenge in retirement is that none of us knows how long we will live for, how our lives will change or what our investment returns will be. Therefore, we must focus on maximising the probability of success in an environment of significant uncertainty.

There are any number of 'rules' or 'approaches' that suggest everything from an age-based allocation to low-risk assets, decreasing growth assets as you age or drawing the same percentage from your portfolio every year. Ultimately, there is no perfect answer.

This is the big paradox of retirement: many people assume that they will build up their retirement kitty through their working life and then draw it down gradually over their retirement, but this is not the way it works in practice. Given the average super balance upon retirement, and given increasing life expectancies, retired people will need to have significant allocations to growth assets such as shares.

If retirement is going to last three to four decades for you – and you will not just be living longer but living a healthier and more active life – your initial spending calculations will need rethinking. If you are drawing down your savings, you risk running out of money if you are too defensive. A strategy that keeps your portfolio growing is crucial to fund your desired lifestyle. That means we all need to invest in growth assets. These include international and domestic shares, property, infrastructure and alternative assets.

Did you know that up to 60 per cent of your investment earnings can come from post-retirement returns? Global investment consulting firm Russell Investments has outlined the 15/35/50 Retirement Lifestyle Rule, whereby the total value of an individual investor's cumulative retirement income should come from the following sources:

- 15 per cent from money saved during an investor's working years
- 35 per cent from the investment growth realised before retirement
- 50 per cent from investment growth that occurs during retirement.

While you may balk at the volatility that continuing share market exposure brings to your retirement experience, the returns that growth assets generate will be an important contributor to replenishing balances as they are drawn down and helping to grow the invested amount. This can be the difference between a comfortable retirement and challenging retirement.

How do retired people invest, and how should they invest?

There are several widely used strategies for investing in retirement and apportioning assets to generate expected outcomes. You may remember the 'buckets' approach we discussed in Chapter 3, which involves dedicating certain assets to certain discrete portions of the portfolio, with the asset types in each bucket representing the short-term, intermediate and long-term timeframes and performing different income-generating or growth-focused roles. Another popular approach in retirement investing is 'lifecycle' or 'age-based' investment – an approach that automatically tailors your investment mix to your age (or how long the investor has until they expect to retire) with the aim of helping you retire with more. Your asset allocation becomes more defensive as you get older and rely more on your investments to replace your income.

The idea behind lifecycle investments is that younger investors have a long time until they retire and should be comfortable taking on more investment risk, the expectation being that they will achieve higher investment returns. However, in the years leading up to retirement, investors naturally become more focused on preserving their capital and so are prepared to lower their investment risk by reducing their exposure to growth assets, instead switching more of their superannuation savings into defensive assets such as bonds and cash. (Lifecycle funds are sometimes known as 'glidepath' funds, because the planned, gradual shift toward lower-risk investments is known as the 'glidepath'.)

Lifecycle funds were included as a default retirement investment option in Australia in 2014. They are offered by both not-for-profit and retail super funds and now make up almost half of all MySuper products. However, lifecycle investing is not without drawbacks. Most obviously, retirement is a highly individual experience, and one size does not fit all. An age-based approach is inherently simplistic; a lifecycle fund largely assumes that people of the same age have similar circumstances and investment objectives, which might not always be the case. Simply shifting a portfolio away from 'growth' assets such as equities to 'defensive' assets such as cash and bonds can, depending on the valuation cycle, not only fail to reduce risk but actually increase it. In cases when bond valuations are at extreme highs, a shift from equities to more 'defensive' bonds could in fact increase the risk of the portfolio without boosting the prospects of improved returns.

A specialist retirement adviser, on the other hand, will weigh up many elements of your personal situation, such as you and your spouse's total wealth, home ownership status, health, age pension eligibility, risk capacity and tolerance, future liabilities, likely spending priorities and behaviour over time and so on to determine an appropriate course of action for you.

Among the biggest misconceptions for many entering retirement is the concept that their retirement capital should continue to grow, or at least be preserved. In fact, the entire system is made to ensure you draw every dollar from the super environment throughout your lifetime.

The golden rules for investing in retirement

A retirement portfolio must be resilient to economic outcomes, recessions, volatility and unexpected events. That means it must be 'anti-fragile'. Retirement portfolios should aim to generate a stable income, preserve capital and achieve some level of growth, if for nothing more than to manage longevity risks.

Having advised hundreds of families through some of the most challenging decisions and periods of their lives, and many thousands more through our podcasts and events, we have come up with something of a 'secret sauce' for investing in retirement. We call this sauce our 'golden rules' to investing in retirement.

1. Define the game you are playing

The explosion of content on the internet, combined with the clickbait focus of many finance and investment media publications, means it is easy for all of us to get caught up in the most popular investments and opportunities. Too often we see the top-performing funds or ETFs of the prior year getting the most inflows in the current year and then ultimately tanking.

The only way to avoid this emotion-driven decision-making is to know your objective, or the 'why' of your retirement strategy, and sticking to it. For most, this is a base-level of income and a reasonable level of capital growth. If you are seeking a consistent income, your first port of call should be the lowest-risk investments on offer: cash and term deposits. If it isn't possible to achieve your desired income through these assets, then some additional risk is likely required. At the centre of our approach is the idea that retired investors should not take on more risk than they need in the pursuit of returns.

This also extends to comparing your experience to those around you. Chats at the golf club or at a BBQ are unlikely to represent the true experience of those you are speaking with, and hence must be taken with a grain of salt and not become a source of envy.

2. Accept that things will go wrong

We know from experience that everything doesn't need to go right for our clients to achieve their objectives. The case study at the beginning of this chapter evidences this.

Daniel may have made the worst possible decision at the worst possible time, but there is always a chance to make a comeback. Subsequent to this decision, Daniel's adviser was able to support him stepping his portfolio back into growth assets to ensure he eventually benefited from the opportunity to recover.

Even the most successful fund managers in the world are wrong as often as 40 per cent of the time, but despite this they are able to deliver strong long-term returns. Your role and that of your adviser should be to minimise the number and severity of the mistakes that are made over your lifetime, but also to keep perspective and remember they will happen.

The return from a portfolio is simply the sum of its parts, and we know that if every investment in a portfolio is performing well at the same time then it is not truly diversified. Every year there will be mistakes, but above-average returns are still achievable for those with the patience to stay invested.

3. Don't bet your house on the base case

There is an old quote that says a forecast tells you more about the forecaster than about the future, and we agree. Central to a retirement-focused investment approach is the knowledge that things can and will go wrong, and that to ensure you are able to navigate all conditions you will need to mitigate what you don't and can't know.

By no means does this mean that you need to be contrarian and do the opposite of everyone else all the time. Rather, you should consider the entire array of potential outcomes and stress-test your portfolio against them, rebalancing accordingly. This is the only way to build a portfolio that is resilient to multiple outcomes.

4. Income plus growth equals total return

'Income plus growth equals total return' may well be the simplest but most forgotten equation in investing.

Too often, we focus solely on the income from investments and forget about the real reason you are investing in them: to deliver a sustainable, growing return over the long term, as retirement is very much a long-term proposition. The only way to achieve both a sustainable and growing income is to invest in companies and assets that are investing in themselves, or more broadly to ensure the capital base is growing.

Psychologically, you need to separate the income produced by your investments from the money you spend to have any hope of a happy retirement. Dividends are inconsistent and paid only twice per year, meaning they are lumpy, and so your focus turns to managing the 'cash flow' that you require rather than just the income.

History has shown that those companies paying the largest dividends often fail to reinvest in themselves and are ultimately found to be dividend 'traps'. In an environment of higher inflation, and with most people investing for at least ten years, fighting the long-term impact of inflation on purchasing power must be central to your approach.

5. Be agnostic to product

Too often we become infatuated with one product or another, whether that be ETFs, managed funds, property or lending. Investments should selected based on their suitability and the exposure they provide you to the prevailing market conditions rather than inherent, existing biases.

You should always be agnostic to product; that is, invest in whatever gives you the best exposure to what you are looking for. Whenever a new investment idea is identified – for example, the Australian share markets look cheap, or the technology sector appears poised for growth due to a focus on AI advancements – your default should be to seek a 'passive' or low-cost option and determine if this is appropriate. If not, then seek advice to understand what type of product is suited to that particular market, sector or asset class and invest accordingly.

6. Smooth the ride

When investing for retirement, the 'average' return is never enough. Investing all of your capital into index-tracking investments means you are subject to the day-to-day whims of share markets. For example, if the S&P/ASX 200 index drops 30 per cent, your domestic shares lose 30 per cent.

As you have access to only a finite pool of capital, the only way to achieve true diversification is to include both passive and actively managed investments, 'active' management referring to those investments whereby a fee is paid in the hope of achieving returns that are better than the market. Active management can help diversify investments, mitigate negative market returns and, if utilised correctly, drive above-market returns.

While most actively managed funds actually underperform their benchmarks over the long-term, they can potentially smooth the ride for investors as they tend to fall less than the market in periods of volatility while outperforming during periods of strength. The key is to make sure managers do more than just track the index.

7. Consider asset allocation paramount

Most investors' attention tends to veer towards the 'sexy' part of investing: stock-picking or investment selection. It is far more exciting and emotionally rewarding to 'pick a winner' than it is to spend time considering the more complex issues associated with asset allocation.

That said, there is no shortage of academic research showing that asset allocation, rather than investment selection, is the biggest contributor to long-term compounding returns. Asset allocation refers to the process of making investments across the three key asset classes: cash, shares and bonds. Asset allocation is estimated to contribute as much 90 per cent to long-term returns for most portfolios.

In retirement, asset allocation takes on a greater level of importance as you must manage a finite pool of capital. In this context, the resilience of a portfolio is central to its success, with resilience only being possible by combining a range of assets that work alongside each other to counter the good and the bad of each asset.

Asset allocation is key to smoothing the volatility that comes with investing and reduces the likelihood of investors making emotional decisions.

8. Remember that beta is free

While it may sound like a complex concept, 'beta' simply refers to the 'index' or 'market' return for an asset class. In the context of shares, that is the return generated by the S&P/ASX 200, the daily fluctuation of which is reported every night on the news.

Investors should not pay high fees to simply gain the average market return. Knowing what you are buying when investing into ETFs, funds or any other asset class is crucial to ensuring you build an efficient portfolio of assets.

In a world where beta is free, it is the selection of this beta that is important. That is, are you choosing Australian shares or international shares, the financial sector or the property sector, and the Nasdaq or the Dow Jones? Likely even more important is asking the question as to whether the 'average' market return alone is something you are comfortable with.

9. Embrace the power of rebalancing

Given the increasing divergence of the global economy and markets, there are significant opportunities to improve returns by making 'tactical' or medium-term allocations to more attractive sectors, asset classes, countries and styles.

Every holding within a portfolio must be able to have a real impact on returns. Thus, we apply a number of simple rules, including the need for the size of individual holdings to exceed one per cent of the total portfolio and the removal or topping-up of any investments that fall to half of the average holding size of the portfolio. Similarly, in strong-performing portfolios we are proponents of regular rebalancing at the asset allocation and investment level – for example, selling a portion of your global share investments following a period in which they have done well to buy assets that haven't performed as well, such as property or bonds. Rebalancing ensures that the portfolio remains aligned with your risk profile and is able to navigate varying market conditions, but also that you are always 'buying low and selling high'.

In Chapter 11, we highlight our 'golden rules' to the navigating the emotional side of retirement. First, though, let's consider some free kicks you can get in your retirement.

Action points

1. Using the budget from prior chapters, now is the time to add 'discretionary' expenses you expect in retirement, such as travel, caravans and golf memberships, and work out how much income you really need.

2. If you have an adviser, ask them for the full cost of your portfolio and to explain the purpose of every individual investment you own.

3. On a single page, review every share, ETF, super fund and property that you own and write next to it either I (income) or G (growth). Is it held to provide an income or for growth, or both?

8

Free kicks

Sally and Sarah Smith are both 50. They met while they were studying together at university and have a daughter, who has recently left home for university. Sally is still working fulltime at a law firm. Sarah is an accountant but has just gone part-time at her accounting firm as she has enrolled in an arts degree. They don't plan to retire for some time yet, but they are starting to research and talk about their plans. In doing so, they have learned of a number of 'free kicks' they think they might be able to take advantage of.

Sarah is working just one day a week, and as her salary is less than $37,000 Sally is able to make an annual superannuation contribution of $3000 on her behalf and receive a $540 tax offset. Now, $540 may not seem like much, but if Sally does it for the next 10 years (assuming they retire at 60) that's an extra $5400 in Sarah's superannuation fund that she wouldn't have had otherwise and for which Sally gets a tax deduction. In addition, Sarah is eligible for the maximum amount of the Australian Government's co-contribution, which means if she makes a personal non-concessional contribution of $1000 to her super then the government will pay an additional $500.

Meanwhile, Sally has been talking to their financial adviser about moving out of her old corporate superannuation fund into the same fund as Sarah, which has much lower costs. She also wants to ask her adviser about the percentage-based fee he has been charging for advice that hasn't changed terribly much in the decade she has been seeing him, during which their investments – and therefore his fee – have grown substantially. If he won't agree to a more reasonable fixed fee, Sally is prepared to look for an adviser who will.

Combined, these 'free kicks' mean that the couple will be able to boost their superannuation by an additional $2000 to $3000 a year. That's an extra $30,000 to $40,000 if they both retire at 65, which is definitely not an amount to be sneezed at, especially when investment earnings are added on top of that!

The Australian superannuation and taxation systems can seem very complex and confusing to people who do not deal with them on a daily basis, but there are lots of hidden tips and tricks that you can take advantage of, like Sally and Sarah have, to make a meaningful impact on your retirement. Free kicks, little wins, freebies, perks, windfalls, bonuses – call them what you will, but anywhere you can gain or keep a dollar is important for saving for your retirement. These tactics become even more vital once you retire and are no longer earning an income.

Here are some strategies to make sure you can score all the free kicks available to you.

Thirties and forties

Superannuation is rarely front of mind when you're in your thirties and forties, but there are some free kicks this age bracket can take advantage of that will make a big difference come retirement.

Co-contribution

As the case study at the beginning of this chapter showed, if you earn less than $43,000, or perhaps have a child who does, then the Australian Government will pay up to $500 a year to match non-concessional (after-tax) superannuation contributions of up to $1000, which is effectively a matching rate of 50 cents on the dollar. Even if you earn up to $58,445 you may be eligible for a small co-contribution.

You don't have to be young to be earning less than the upper threshold of $58,445, as was the case with Sarah, who was 50. One day a week could potentially mean having your after-tax contributions matched.

Tthe ATO does not require you to apply for this co-contribution. As it states on its website: 'When you lodge your tax return, we will work out if you're eligible. If your super fund has your tax file number (TFN), we will pay it to your super account automatically'.

Consolidating superannuation accounts

This free kick applies to people of all ages. It is not unusual to have more than one superannuation account, especially if you have been in the workforce for decades, but with each superannuation fund comes fees and charges that you should only be paying once. You could also be being charged for multiple life insurance policies. These amounts can add up over the decades.

The Your Future, Your Super reforms introduced super stapling in November 2021. This requires employees to be 'stapled' to their super fund regardless of where they work, which has reduced the incidence of multiple superannuation accounts. However, this legislation is still relatively new, and there are plenty of people out there with multiple accounts.

ATO Online Services will have a record of your superannuation balances across all your superannuation funds if your funds have your TFN. You can see these balances through Services Australia's online portal myGov if you have linked to ATO Online Services. You can also call the ATO's super search line on 13 28 65 and provide personal details, including TFN, date of birth, visa holder status (if applicable), details of the super fund where contributions may have been made and previous personal and employment details. Finally, you can complete a 'Searching for lost super' form (available at ato.gov.au/forms-and-instructions/superannuation-searching-for-lost-superannuation) and return it to the ATO via post.

Once you have located all your superannuation funds, make sure you consolidate them into the one fund. This should be easy enough to do by completing forms provided by your super fund, or your financial adviser can help.

Concessional contributions

Superannuation is one of the most concessionally taxed vehicles available. Unless you are earning less than $18,201 ($21,885 with the low-income tax offset) and therefore not being taxed at all on your income, the tax rate of 15 per cent in super will always be better than the tax rate on your earnings. (People on incomes of $250,000 or more, including superannuation, will need to pay Division 293 tax, or an extra 15 per cent, on the amount exceeding $250,000.) So, it is in your best tax interests to make concessional contributions when you can. In Chapter 6, we explained in detail how to make concessional contributions and who they are best suited to, but being able to cut your tax rate to 15 per cent is a free kick in anyone's language.

As we explained in Chapter 6, there are limits on how much you can contribute concessionally into your super each year. The ATO does this to make sure people don't take advantage of the lower tax rate in super. However, unused cap amounts can be carried forward for up to five years before they expire if your total super balance is less than $500,000 at the end of the prior financial year. You can find out your unused cap amount by checking ATO services via myGov.

Refreshing your superannuation fund

Superannuation has changed a great deal over the decades, and so have the funds that look after your retirement savings. Not only is it a good idea to find any lost superannuation, but you could potentially save money by examining the superannuation fund you are using, especially if you haven't given it a thought for some years.

If you are still with a corporate or employer superannuation plan, or a closed Choice product, that you joined in the 2000s, have a look at your statement and examine the fees and charges you are incurring. In an examination of Choice superannuation products for 2021–22 financial year, APRA found that average fees are higher in Choice products that are closed to new members. The average annual administration fee for members with an account balance of $50,000 in closed Choice products was $225, compared with $149 for open Choice products and $137 for MySuper products. Unfortunately, old products that were closed to new members were also more likely to underperform the benchmark, making it doubly important to ensure your super fund is being responsible with your savings.

If your super is invested via a platform product – a corporate super fund under which your assets are pooled with others' for greater scale – you may want to check that you are not being charged extra for each managed fund that your super is being directed into.

By picking up all these extra fees and charges, and moving your retirement savings into a more modern fund, you could potentially save hundreds or even thousands of dollars a year and make a significant addition to your retirement income.

Spouse contribution

Another strategy that is available to couples if one is earning significantly less than the other is a tax offset for a spouse superannuation contribution. This is a good tool to use if one partner is taking time off work to raise children, but there are many cases in which it can be applied. Sally and Sarah in the case study at the beginning of this chapter no longer had children at home, but because Sarah had gone back to part time work while she studied and was on an income of less than $37,000, Sally was able to make an annual superannuation contribution of $540 on her behalf for which she received a tax offset.

The offset is eligible for spouses earning up to $40,000.

Spouse tax offset

The tax offset is calculated as 18 per cent of the lesser of:

- $3000 minus the amount over $37,000 that the spouse earns
- the value of the spouse contributions.

There are some other eligibility requirements. For example, the spouse must be under 75 years old for the 2020–21 income years and later, and the spouse cannot exceed their non-concessional contributions cap in the income year in which the contribution is made. The spouse also needs to have a total super balance less than the general transfer balance cap ($1.9 million as at 1 July 2023) immediately before the start of the income year in which the contribution is made.

Fifties

Here are some strategies that you can implement as you get closer to the end of your career.

Hidden fees

As you hit your fifties, you should probably start getting a bit more forensic with how you review your annual superannuation fund statements. If you've followed our advice from earlier in this chapter, you should have moved your funds from any legacy products into better-performing options, but now you need to step it up a notch.

You need to consider whether your funds are doing the best they can where they are. If your super platform has a portion of your funds in a cash option, what is the cash rate they are paying? If the interest is negligible, which is unfortunately often the case, would your cash funds be better off elsewhere? If the rate is less than 1 per cent, whereas outside of super you would be getting at least 3 per cent, you should really consider moving at least some of those funds.

Also, find out if you are being classified as a 'wholesale' investor (see Chapter 4). While often wholesale fees may be cheaper than retail fees for investment products, make sure you are not being charged 'placement fees' as this can be expensive and unnecessary.

Self-insurance

If you are over 55, are debt-free with no mortgage on any of your properties and have significant financial assets, then you might want to seriously question the value of your insurance. This includes privately held insurance and life and total and permanent disability insurance via your SMSF. With the cost of insurance premiums rising, you might want to ask yourself why you are paying potentially tens of thousands of dollars a year to cover yourself for events that rarely happen when you have sufficient funds to cover any losses yourself.

It's a different story, of course, if you're younger with dependent young children and mortgages that you need to keep paying. However, once the kids have left home and you're in the fortunate position of paying off your residence, seriously consider the benefits of cancelling excess insurance policies.

Percentage versus fixed fees

A common fee model for providing financial advice is a percentage of the assets under management. Clients with more money to invest would therefore be paying more in overall fees.

Advocates of asset-based percentage fees say clients with more funds have more complex situations and therefore take up more of their advisers' time, but this is rarely the case, as Sarah and Sally found in the example at the beginning of this chapter. The advice they were receiving had barely changed in the decade they had been receiving it, although the benefit to the adviser had definitely grown as their assets had grown.

We would argue that it doesn't cost an adviser ten times more of their time or skills for ten times more in investible capital. If you are using an adviser who is charging this way, discuss with them how this is creating value for you and why a fixed annual fee of a dollar amount wouldn't be more appropriate. If they won't engage with you about this, seriously consider taking your business to somebody who will. It could mean a return to your super fund of thousands of dollars a year.

Sixties and over

Here are some strategies that you can implement on the cusp of retirement and beyond.

Re-contribution

A re-contribution strategy can leave tax-free benefits for your dependants. There may be no obvious benefit to you – after all, you are simply withdrawing a lump sum and then recontributing it back to super – but the tax status of your superannuation will definitely matter to your dependants, whether that be your spouse or your children, when you die.

Your superannuation has taxable and tax-free components. The tax-free components are the contributions you have made from after-tax monies – usually non-concessional contributions. Seeing as how all superannuation withdrawals are tax-free once you reached age 60 and have met a condition of release, such as leaving a job, you can simply withdraw a lump sum and then put the money back into super. If you do not claim a tax deduction for it, that proportion of the super would move from taxable to non-taxable. You still need to keep in mind your non-concessional contribution limits, but you can package up three years of non-concessional contributions caps, or $330,000, into one year. You also need to be under age 75 and have a total superannuation balance of less than

$1.68 million on 30 June of the previous financial year to be able to use the bring-forward rule.

The more of your super you can shift from taxable to non-taxable, the better off your beneficiaries will be when you pass on.

Commonwealth Seniors Health Card

If have reached age pension eligibility – 67 years old if you were born on 1 January 1957 or later – and meet certain eligibility criteria, you should be able to apply for the Commonwealth Seniors Health Card, which provides a variety of benefits, including cheaper medicines under the Pharmaceutical Benefits Scheme (PBS), bulk-billed doctor visits (depending on your doctor) and a refund for medical costs when you reach the Medicare Safety Net. You may also receive free medicines under the PBS when you meet the PBS Safety Net threshold in a year.

Commonwealth Seniors Health Card eligibility income test

To be eligible for the Commonwealth Seniors Health Card, you must earn less than the following in the last financial year:

- $95,400 a year for singles
- $152,640 a year for couples
- $190,800 a year for couples separated by illness, respite care or prison.

Add $639.60 to the above amounts for each child in your care.

Depending on your state or territory and council area, you could also get cheap public transport and discounts on your council rates, water and power.

Not everybody who is eligible applies for it, but a Commonwealth Seniors Health Card could easily save you a few thousand dollars a year – a decent free kick across your retirement.

Franking credits

For retirees operating in a zero-tax-rate environment, imputation credits on franked dividends can now provide you with rebates back into your superannuation fund.

As the tax on these dividends already paid by the company are attributable to you, and as you are no longer paying tax on super fund earnings once you retire if you are over 60, you are entitled to effectively receive the tax refund back into your super. To get your refund quickly, you need to lodge your tax return as soon as possible after the end of the financial year. Also, you may want to consider investing more into products that issue franking credits given the rebates you will receive.

Better deals

Many of us are often paralysed by inertia when it comes to changing any kind of provider, whether that be electricity, internet or accountant, but it can really pay to shop around and see if you can get a better deal from your accountant, SMSF platform or even adviser.

Just as percentage-based fees can become exorbitant when your investments grow, so too can the fees charged by accountants. Just because an accountant is small doesn't necessarily mean their fees will be lower. Call around to providers in your area and some larger firms to make a comparison. If you have a valuable relationship with your current accountant and don't want to lose it, surely they can do you the courtesy of at least having a discussion about fees?

As you move from the accumulation phase to the retirement phase, what you need from your platform provider changes, and so you may need to shop around to get a platform that meets your needs at the best possible cost.

Commence a pension

Once you have made the decision to retire and take your funds, it's important to decide how to take the funds – either as a lump sum or a pension – as soon as possible. The longer you leave any money in accumulation phase, the longer you will be paying tax on its earnings.

In Chapter 6 our case study looked at Joan Stone, recently retired at 66, who had left $100,000 in accumulation phase. If that $100,000 managed to return 8 per cent while she was waiting to use it – or $8000 – it would incur a tax bill of $1200 that she could have avoided if she had withdrawn it or shifted it into a pension.

The '2023 Annual Benchmark Report' from SMSF administrative provider Class found that compared to large APRA-regulated funds, people with SMSFs were far more likely to commence a pension once they reached retirement age. As the simple example of Joan highlights, the financial ramifications of not starting a pension can be real and significant the longer you wait.

Seniors discounts

In addition to the Commonwealth Seniors Health Card, each state and territory offers their own seniors card, which comes with a suite of benefits and discounts across transport, utilities and even holiday attractions. In Victoria, for example, there is the free travel voucher program under which seniors can register for two to four free travel vouchers a year. In New South Wales, discounts include reduced petrol at certain retailers, discounts on delivery at Woolworths and 50 per cent off adoption rates for senior animals (more than 8 years old) from the RSPCA. You are also eligible for the gold Opal card, which entitles you to travel on the Opal public transport network for $2.50 a day.

Your state or territory government's website will usually have a directory of senior card discounts where you can search by area, or a downloadable directory of your area that outlines the discounts available. You may be eligible for your state or territory's seniors card before you are eligible for the Commonwealth Seniors Health Card as you often only need to be 60 and working less than a certain amount of hours per week.

Action points

1. Check your tax return(s) for last financial year to see if you or your partner are eligible for the Australian Government's co-contribution. This requires an income below $58,445.

2. Grab your super fund's annual member statement and head to the APRA website (apra.gov.au) to check how you fund stacked up on the performance test.

3. If you are pension age with an income below $95,400 for singles or $152,640 for couples, apply for the Commonwealth Seniors Health Card. If you are under pension age, call your bank, lender and insurer and ask for a better deal on your mortgage, car loan or bank account. It never hurts to ask.

9
Managing market anxiety

Christine and Charlie are both 70 and have been retired for 10 years. They both worked full-time jobs for most of their life and were able to retire on a combined superannuation balance that allows them to take an annual income of $150,000. They own their home plus a holiday apartment on the Gold Coast and have been enjoying the early years of their retirement.

However, as their retirement nest egg has reduced, Christine has become increasingly worried about whether or not they will run out of money. They take a monthly income via an allocated pension, and Christine also wants to leave decent inheritances for their two daughters and their grandchildren. She didn't pay much attention to markets during her working life when she was employed as a psychologist, but following the events of 2020 and the market volatility that occurred during COVID-19 she has started to monitor their retirement savings on an almost daily basis. She is also constantly pestering Charlie to speak to their financial adviser about what is in their portfolio and wants to sell down shares she thinks are too risky.

Charlie, on the other hand, is more sanguine about market volatility and how it will impact their retirement funds. He was previously a manager in a large bank and has been hearing about market volatility for as long as he can remember. He thinks it's his familiarity with markets that makes him less nervous about their nest egg. He is worried about his wife, though, and so they schedule an in-person meeting with their financial adviser to help her allay her anxiety.

Fortunately, their financial planner is more than sympathetic to Christine's concerns and takes the time to explain market volatility and the importance of patience when it comes to investing in equity markets. Critically, their adviser is not condescending and takes the time to listen to both Christine and Charlie. The adviser reworks their strategy slightly so that Christine is better able to sleep at night without overly compromising returns.

Worrying for all the wrong reasons

Running out of money before you die is not an unreasonable fear to have in retirement. In fact, results from the 2023 National Seniors Social Survey indicated that one in five participants frequently worry about outliving their savings and investments, and over half agreed that they worried either frequently or occasionally. However, this worry, and the anxiety around market volatility and investment performance that it links to, can have seriously detrimental effects on retirement savings if people rush into decisions at the height of their anxiety.

To highlight the hit that moving out of markets at the wrong time can have, let's look at what would have happened if a retiree had shifted all their money to cash at the bottom of the market in 2020, for example, and not invested for another 10 months.

On 16 March 2020 the S&P/ASX 200 recorded its biggest one-day fall on record of 9.7 per cent, at which point it was at 30 per cent off the peak it reached on 21 February that year. If at that point a retiree shifted their whole portfolio – which was worth $100,000 at the peak of the market on 21 February – to cash, they would solidify losses of 30 per cent, or $30,000.

If, however, that investor had done nothing that year – that is, they had not checked their balances daily and were confident in the asset allocation they had chosen, or their adviser had chosen for them – the end result would have been very different. A portfolio invested in the ASX/S&P 200 that was worth $100,000 on 1 January 2020, would have been worth $103,950 at the end of January the following year.

That's a $30,000 loss for acting on market anxiety versus a small gain for doing nothing.

The long game

The Vanguard Index Chart (vanguard.com.au/personal/support/index-chart) shows what an investment of $10,000 in various asset classes would look like 30 years later. The 2023 version (the version available at the time of writing) highlights that even with major market corrections – such as that of the dot-com bubble in 2001, the global financial crisis (GFC) in 2007 and the more recent COVID-19 fall in 2020 – investments in markets grow exponentially over time, and most asset classes grow at a vastly greater rate than cash. It quantifies in dollar figures the cost of acting on market anxiety.

Telling somebody not to worry about markets and actually getting them not to worry about markets are two different things. Christine, on one level, is very aware of how damaging her market anxiety can be. As a psychologist, she worked for years with clients who had major anxiety issues, and so she knows that while a healthy level of anxiety can be helpful, when it starts to consume someone's life or keep them awake at night it can become truly damaging.

She found her and Charlie's visit to the financial planner particularly helpful because the adviser took her concerns seriously. They didn't belittle her or condescend to her, things her husband thankfully hasn't done either. Rather, the financial planner went through the couple's current investments across the various asset classes they are invested in, showed them long-term investment return charts like the Vanguard Index Chart and explained the risk–reward characteristics of each asset class.

Christine appreciated the financial planner's PowerPoint presentation because it made her realise that as safe as cash is, its long-term returns really pale in comparison with something like Australian shares. She now understands that if they were to shift all their retirement funds to cash at the expense of better-performing asset classes, they would be taking on another kind of risk.

She would like to slightly increase the cash allocation and, together with Charlie and their planner Ali, has worked out a number that would make her feel more comfortable than she currently does. This small rebalance, along with the respect she was shown in these discussions, means that Christine is getting a much better night's sleep and has stopped her daily checking of their super balance.

Diversification

In Chapter 7 we looked at investing in retirement, and examined asset allocation and why it's important not to put all your investment eggs in one basket. We discussed how individual approaches to asset allocation will probably change over time and during certain major life events.

Along with overall outperformance, one of the benefits of good asset allocation is reducing portfolio risk. If your investments are diversified across and within a variety of different asset classes, then if volatility hits one asset class your other holdings should protect you. This approach to investing is called modern portfolio theory (MPT) and was put forward by Harry Markowitz in a paper in 1952. It may seem like common sense, but it hasn't always been accepted market wisdom. MPT says that every investment comes with a certain level of risk and return. High-return investments are often high risk, and low-risk investments are often low return. However, a combination of both kinds of investments can help elevate an overall portfolio's return while maintaining an acceptable level of risk.

For example, in Australia the financial and banking sector is particularly large, and it's not uncommon for investors' portfolios to be overweighted towards the big four banks – NAB, CBA, ANZ and Westpac. While these are good blue chip companies and their profits have certainly delivered for shareholders, if these were the only companies you held in your retirement SMSF you would be incredibly exposed to volatility in that sector. Similarly, if your SMSF only had one or two commercial properties in it, you can imagine how exposed it would be to movements in the property market compared to if it also had investments in equities (both global and domestic), fixed income, cash and perhaps some private equity.

Having a good understanding of how diversification can protect your investments as well as maximising returns can help in alleviating market anxiety.

Liquidity

If you are in the retirement phase and paying yourself a pension, then liquidity – the ability to quickly and easily convert assets into cash – is very important. Knowing that you can access funds when you need them is another way to reduce anxiety.

In addition to being overly concentrated, an SMSF or retirement portfolio with just one commercial property asset in it does not offer good levels of liquidity. If you needed funds, you would have to sell the property, and a quick sale is not guaranteed. Holding your business real property in your SMSF and renting it back to your business might seem like a sound strategy, but depending on how niche your business is and what the property does, be mindful of how difficult it could be to sell the property.

Any good investment strategy should have a reasonable allocation to cash, but keep in mind the liquidity differences between equities, real property and even some managed funds. During the GFC some investors got caught up in managed funds that they could not get out of for some time because of liquidity issues, so it's very important that you read the fine print of product disclosure documents before you invest.

Cost versus peace

Different strategies come with different costs depending on what is involved. There are many low-cost ETFs and index funds available to investors, but these can often be more volatile than more actively managed strategies.

The more active a strategy, the more a fund manager is likely to charge for it, but don't forget what you are paying for. The fund manager will be taking a day-to-day interest in the fund's investments and conducting vast amounts of research and due diligence on each investment in the fund. They will not always be right, but it may be worth paying more for active management, especially if it is offering some downside protection for your funds as well (that is, protection against decreases in the value of your investments). The 'sleep at night' factor could be priceless.

Rebalancing

Portfolio diversification is important to reduce market risk and anxiety, but you will also need to rebalance your portfolio at least annually and potentially after major market events. Rebalancing is essentially a reset to make sure your portfolio is constantly reflective of your asset allocation goals. It will be required when, for example, a particular share or sector rises in value over a period of time and therefore represents a much larger portion of your portfolio than you wanted it to originally. In this case you may need to sell some of those shares and reallocate the funds to other investments in the portfolio.

If you don't attend to rebalancing, you may become overly exposed to risky assets. Say a portfolio is invested 50/50 in growth assets and defensive assets; if the growth assets triple in value, then that portfolio is now weighted 75/25 towards growth assets and is therefore much more exposed to generally more high-risk assets.

Market anxiety game plan

1. Understand your investment strategy.
2. Understand the importance of diversification and how it offers protection.
3. Understand your risk profile and align it with your partner's.
4. Sleep at night.

What is your risk profile?

Your risk profile is a measure of the level of risk you are comfortable with. It is sometimes called the 'sleep at night' test – it doesn't really matter if your investments have the potential for incredible returns if they don't let you sleep. Risk profiles often change over time as people's circumstances evolve. Your risk profile as a young adult will likely be very different to your risk profile as a retiree. Christine, for example, became more risk-averse the older she got and the more reliant she became on their retirement savings to live on.

Double trouble with couple profiles

Many couples run into trouble when they have very different risk profiles. A defensive person with an aggressive-risk-profile spouse will be in for some very anxious evenings. Likewise, the partner with the aggressive risk profile might become increasingly frustrated with their other half's reluctance to take on what they believe are reasonable investment risks for superior returns.

For these reasons, it's probably best that each person in a partnership complete their own risk profile first and then compare them to understand where the differences lie. Once the differences are understood, it is easier to put together an investment strategy that takes into account both attitudes. This is especially important if approaches to risk are very different.

If one party in the couple has had most of the responsibility for financial decisions during the relationship, they may not even be aware of their partner's approach to risk. With communication problems being one of the most common reasons for divorce in Australia, according to The State of Relationships lawyer survey by Australian Family Lawyers, it is important that couples get on the same page when it comes to risk as they head into retirement.

This was very important for Charlie and Christine, whose relationship was becoming increasingly fraught as they headed into what should have been a comfortable and pleasant retirement. Looking into their risk profiles and having a discussion with their financial adviser – who took both their concerns seriously – has done wonders for their marriage.

The main thing

Ultimately, the most important part of any investment strategy is to gain the benefit of compounding as investment returns accrue each year. Thus, any good investment strategy should be focused on limiting volatility and helping to make sound, informed decisions that are not dictated by emotions.

Understanding how and why you react to certain investment situations is key to keeping any market anxiety you might have in check, as is knowing your risk profile. With this information in hand, you should be able to formulate an investment strategy that not only maximises your returns – within an acceptable level of risk – but also allows you to sleep at night.

Action points

1. Determine how risk-aware or risk-averse you are.
2. With the help of a financial adviser or online resources, separate each of your assets into high, medium and low risk and compare how your allocation fits with your risk profile.
3. Write down each of the investments or assets you own today that you would with certainty buy again tomorrow regardless.

10

The mistakes we make

At the very beginning of this book, in Chapter 1, we met Simon and Yoshi, who had very different approaches to retirement that ended up having significant consequences on their standard of living. Yoshi and his wife Jane had done a lot of research and groundwork leading up to their sixties and found themselves in rather an enviable position as they began their retirement journey. Simon, on the other hand, appeared to have made a number of rash decisions or 'mistakes'. He and his spouse Jan were facing the potential of life in later retirement on a restricted income because of early spending decisions made in the 'honeymoon' period of retirement. The decisions Simon made could be interpreted as mistakes, but they are easy to make, and Simon and Jan are definitely not the first to make them.

By reading this book, we hope you are now in a much better position to face retirement, no matter your life stage. As outlined in the previous chapters, you can make significant decisions in your forties, fifties and even sixties that will mean you have a much more comfortable life once you stop working.

In this chapter, we examine many of the common mistakes that people can make in retirement and how to avoid them. Fortunately, most of the 'corrections' to these mistakes have been outlined in previous chapters.

General mistakes

There are a number of general mistakes that people can make when it comes to retirement planning. Many of these involve people's attitudes and beliefs, which are, fortunately, relatively easy to fix if you have the right mindset.

Avoiding financial education

In Chapter 4, we looked at the role of financial literacy, or understanding financial matters. Australians appear to be relatively financially literate according to the Australian Government's National Financial Capability Survey 2021, which found that our average financial literacy score was 68 out of 100, but there are still some people who do not make the effort to understand the basic principles of business and finance.

Some people decide to hand all of their financial and retirement issues over to professionals, and while professionals have very important roles to play, to understand whether or not you are picking the right ones you still need to have a basic level of knowledge around superannuation and other basic financial issues.

For a start, you need to be able to ask the right questions of your financial adviser. If you don't know what diversification or asset allocation are (both of which are explained in Chapter 7), how will you be able to ask your financial planner about their proposed investment strategy? If you don't understand your risk profile (see Chapter 9), how will you know whether you are comfortable with an investment strategy suggested for you?

Not having a basic level of financial education also makes you more susceptible to scams. Investment scams include relationship and romance baiting scams, but they also include money recovery services or businesses purporting to be able to get money back from a scam, as well as dodgy IPO scams and imposter bond scams. As scammers get increasingly more sophisticated, you need to be as financially literate as possible to ensure you are not caught up in a scheme that completely erodes your retirement savings.

Not getting the basics right

Another mistake that people make, which leads on from inadequate financial literacy, is not doing the right groundwork. Maximising your superannuation can be done throughout your life, and the earlier you understand its importance, the bigger the benefits will be.

In an ideal world, everyone would take an interest in their superannuation from the day they first become a member of a fund. That doesn't necessarily mean you have to be making extra contributions as a 20-year-old, although that would obviously help, but just being engaged and becoming interested in your balance from an early age can be incredibly helpful.

A mistake made too often is when people find themselves thinking about their retirement for the first time in their mid-sixties, when it is usually too late for them to make a meaningful difference to their superannuation balance. To avoid becoming that person, consider the different strategies laid out in Chapter 6 to boost superannuation for different age groups, along with the free kicks outlined in Chapter 8, which even some older pre-retirees might be able to use.

Being a cheapskate

As the adage goes, you get what you pay for. If you find a super cheap financial adviser, there is usually a reason they are charging low fees, and it won't be good.

In Chapter 4, we put a checklist together for any financial adviser you might be considering engaging. Regardless of any adviser's proposed fees, if you can't tick all of the boxes, continue your search.

Importantly, you also need to check if they are registered on the ASIC registry at moneysmart.gov.au/financial-advice/financial-advisers-register. Cut-throat fees could be suggestive of a cut-throat approach to everything, including the law.

You should have a set of questions prepared that you ask any professional you are considering, with the key question being how willing they are to explain anything they are proposing for your investments or assets.

Also, there has been a lot of emphasis on low-fee investment options recently, and while these definitely serve a purpose – for the young investor, perhaps, who is looking to build their wealth or save for a house deposit – they often only track a market index. Active management may be more expensive, but you are also paying for a manager's experience in managing investments, which can deliver better returns and protection.

Don't ignore fees

It may seem to run counter to the advice we've just given, but it's important to also question any fee you are being charged and understand what it is for. The key here is to have all fees disclosed. If you don't understand something, always query it. This is just as true if your manager or financial adviser is delivering superior performance as if they are not.

Falling for ego traps

We all have egos, and it can be easy to be caught up by anyone or anything that panders to it. We all like to think that we are 'smart' or 'sophisticated', even if evidence suggests otherwise. And if recent history has shown us anything – for example, through the incredible run in meme stocks during 2020 and 2021 before an ultimate capitulation – just because you might be fortunate enough to have accrued a decent amount of wealth, that doesn't necessarily make you smarter, either.

A trap that people can sometimes get ensnared by is being classified as a 'wholesale client' or 'sophisticated investor', which can lead to them losing some rights. This was a red flag we examined in Chapter 4. Similarly, be aware of any investment scheme or promotion marketed to you as being too complex for you to understand, or 'once in a lifetime' opportunities available only to 'intelligent, lucky people like you'. Always remember that if something sounds too good to be true, it probably is.

Doing it yourself

If you do know a little bit about financial markets and investments, it can be very tempting to try and manage your superannuation and retirement strategy yourself. With average fees for financial advice now in excess of $4000 a year, we understand how appealing this may be. However, you really need to ask yourself, how savvy are you really? For example, how familiar are you with the *Superannuation Industry (Supervision) Act 1993*? Have you even heard of it? Do you know what it does?

Even if you believe you could become au fait with all the superannuation and investment regulations, have you accounted for the time it will take for you to do so? Managing your own affairs is a serious business and will take up a significant portion of your time if you are still employed. Is this time that you would be better off spending on other things?

Your investment professionals also have years of experience in these fields. They understand behavioural finance and why people may sometimes make rash decisions. This is serious expertise that is well worth paying for.

Overestimating the importance of insurance

All our lives we are taught to insure for events and situations that we can't control. A lot of this messaging is important, but a lot of it comes from the insurance industry itself. As important as insuring your home and contents, vehicle and life is, especially when you are younger, as you age you may want to reconsider the level of life insurance coverage you have relative to its cost.

The government made life insurance in superannuation opt-in for people under 25 in 2020 (under the Putting Members' Interests First legislation) for a reason. This is because at that point in people's lives it's more important for superannuation to be accruing than to pay for life insurance premiums you may not need.

As you age, premiums become more expensive and cover may not change that much. In Chapter 8 we examined self-insuring and concluded that if you are over 55, debt-free with no mortgages and have significant financial assets, then it's worth considering self-insurance. This just means you might put enough aside to cover yourself in the event of any calamity instead of continuing to pay exorbitant premiums.

Investment mistakes

Investment mistakes fall into a category of their own as they can have big repercussions when it comes to your nest egg. Putting all your retirement eggs in one investment basket, for example, could mean that your retirement savings disappear entirely if something happens to that basket.

Misunderstanding diversification

As discussed in previous chapters, diversification is key to a good investment strategy. This involves investing across a range of asset classes and a range of investments within those asset classes.

Chapter 7 goes into detail about the basics of asset allocation, but adequate diversification involves investing across all the major asset classes as well as in a number of investments within those asset classes. A mistake some investors make is not to understand the importance of both. For example, somebody might be invested in ten or more Australian equities and think that they are sufficiently diversified, but if you look closer you find that those ten stocks are the four major banks and six other companies in the financial services industry. As these companies are all in the same sector, the investor would not be protected if something happened to this industry.

Similarly, home country bias can be a problem. Australian equity markets represent less than 5 per cent of global equity markets. It can be tempting to invest in what is familiar to you, but by doing so, your portfolio would be missing out on the other 95 per cent of global markets and opportunities. You would also be missing out on the unique opportunities in those markets. For example, any investment in the Nasdaq provides exposure to the likes of Alphabet, Facebook and Tesla, leaders in their fields, which are not available in Australia.

Investing overseas

Too often people make the mistake of thinking that international investments are riskier when in fact the reverse – only investing domestically – can actually be riskier. International equity markets often outperform Australian equity markets, and spreading your investments across different countries provides protection if anything were to happen in just one of those markets.

Trying to time the market

Timing the market involves moving in and out of investments based on what you think those investments will do in the short term. For example, if you had foreseen the GFC and moved out when the market was at its top in 2007, and then successfully predicted the bottom and reinvested, that would be timing the market. But as the book *The Big Short* by Michael Lewis and the subsequent movie highlighted, only a handful of people in the world were able to do that, and it is doubtful whether even they could do it consistently.

Also, those people that did do it, or at least did not buy into the hype surrounding the elevated markets prior to the GFC, have made a career out of examining and researching markets and spend most of their waking hours doing it. For the rest of us who don't have unlimited time to do the same, timing the market is virtually impossible.

It might sound boring but the saying 'Time in the market beats timing the market' is true.

Thinking short-term

Short-termism, or focusing too much on what is happening in the daily headlines, is something we covered in Chapter 9 as it can be a big cause of market anxiety.

If you are investing for your retirement, then you should have a very long-term outlook. As reasonable as it is to worry about running out of money before you die, watching the daily financial news cycle is not going to help you and will most likely just make you worry and lose sleep at night. Your superannuation and retirement strategy involves long-term decisions, and you need to remind yourself that just because something is the headlines today doesn't mean it will be next year or even next week.

In 2023, for example, large language models and generative AI were all the rage, and as innovative and breakthrough as this technology was, you may have thought your portfolio was dead in the water if you didn't have a major allocation to AI. However, if as a serious long-term investor you already had an allocation to technology as part of your overall strategy, you would have been benefiting from those important advancements anyway. It is always important to be diversified across all traditional sectors and industries and seek to avoid the latest craze.

Chasing income

As you shift from the accumulation phase to the retirement phase, your focus will probably shift from building your capital base to the income it can generate. This is totally reasonable. We have covered in previous chapters the very real fear that retirees have of running out of money before they die. This is not an unreasonable fear, but you cannot be guided by this fear alone, especially when it comes to your investment allocation in retirement.

A big mistake that retirees can make when they are focused on income is to shift large sections of their portfolio into investments that focus on generating income. This means a prevalence of property trusts, private credit and loan funds, and while these investment options may deliver superior income, the retiree may unfortunately be forfeiting capital and capital growth as a result. Also, some of these income-generating products can be quite risky, and if investors don't do their due diligence properly they may be investing in products that could make a serious dint in their portfolio if they were to go bust. A good example of this would be the collateralised debt obligations (CDOs) that were so prevalent during the GFC. Investors were hypnotised by the income they were generating and didn't look under the hood at the types of mortgages that were backing them.

In Chapter 7 we looked at appropriate retirement strategies for retirement. There should be no single type of investment you chase as a retiree; instead, focus on the appropriate asset allocation for your risk profile.

Tax-driven investing

Retirees should also avoid focusing on investing for tax purposes alone or being attracted to investments solely for their tax deductibility.

There are plenty of examples of failed managed investment schemes in the agriculture industry that promised their investors incredible returns with tax deductions on some of their initial outlays. Great Southern Group is a good example of this. It was involved in forestry plantations, viticulture, olives and beef, but it eventually collapsed as its underlying agriculture assets underperformed and it was subsidising returns to some investors in its earlier schemes.

In terms of the tax benefits of negative gearing for property investors, as attractive as it is outside of superannuation, it is not so attractive if you have properties in your SMSF because the tax offset only applies to other income your superannuation fund earns, which is concessionally taxed anyway.

There is no secret to success

As much as we would like it to be so, there are no simple rules that will guarantee your success in retirement.

All markets go up or down each year and it is impossible to predict by how much or when. Buy and hold strategies tend to work out best over the long term, but you need to understand the risk–return balance you feel most comfortable with and invest according to that.

We hope that this book will be a useful tool for anyone who is even just a little bit anxious about their retirement plans. And remember, it's not always all about the money – it's just as important to work on your life goals, plans and strategies as you head into retirement as it is to work on your finances.

Action points

1. Write down the five biggest financial or investment mistakes you have made over your lifetime.

2. Buy yourself a copy of the following books, or add them to your Christmas list:
   - *The Psychology of Money* by Morgan Housel
   - *Buying Happiness* by Kate Campbell
   - *Mind over Money* by Evan Lucas.

3. With scams more prevalent than ever, check with each of your bank and investment account providers to ensure that multi-factor authentication is set up.

11

The golden rules for a successful, fulfilling retirement

Retirement, just like life, is what you make it. The ultimate intention of this book is to provide a framework – or, at the very least, some insights – for how you can ensure your retirement is everything you want it to be and more.

More than anything, we hope this book has shown you that while money is important in retirement, it is not the only thing you should worry about. Money may be able to buy happiness, but only up to a point; the rest is up to you.

Everyone will have a different experience in retirement, and yours ultimately comes down to the expectations you set. In this final chapter, we look back at the many case studies and examples drawn from our decades of experience supporting Australians of all ages and distil these into our golden rules for a successful, fulfilling retirement.

Define success

Success in retirement is simple: find what brings you joy and spend more time doing that. Achieving this, however, is among the most difficult tasks you will face in your life.

Why? Because there is no simple recipe or 'right answer' that defines a successful retirement. Having $2 million in your bank account or being able to travel to Europe for three months every year may be one person's definition of success. For someone else, however, this may sound exhausting and the last thing they would wish to do with their spare time.

As advisers who have seen hundreds of families and watched as clients and friends have transitioned through each life stage, our biggest lesson for you is to ensure that you redefine what success means to you. This is particularly difficult for those with successful careers and, unfortunately, it does not always happen overnight.

There is no number or dollar amount of assets that suits everyone. What truly matters is your ability to sleep well at night.

Don't go it alone

Mental health is among the biggest challenges we face as a society. The stoic mindset that is instilled in many older generations, likely caused by the experiences of multiple recessions, means reaching out is even more difficult for those of you in retirement or your latter years.

Retirement is not the time to be too proud to speak up. Don't go it alone in retirement. Now is the time to be building new friendships and finding new hobbies with all that new-found time. Never be afraid to ask for help, as it is entirely natural to find yourself struggling for meaning during such a significant period of your life.

This also extends into the financial side of things, which you may expect to become less complicated once you retire. The taxation and super system in Australia is complex, and obtaining professional advice on key decisions – whether about downsizing, investing or tax – can make sure one bad decision doesn't devastate your retirement.

Ignore the Joneses

'June and Philip have such a nice car; how can they afford that even though we did the same job for the last 30 years?'

In retirement, you can do anything you want – you have complete flexibility. So, don't get stuck on what others are doing. Don't worry that your neighbour has a bigger house, boat or jet ski. Enjoy what you have and find joy in the small things.

The 'Instagram' or 'Facebook' effect is well known – we only ever talk or post about the good things happening in our lives, not the bad. So ignore what the Joneses are posting and move forward with your life.

Nowhere is this more relevant than when it comes to investments, with retirement naturally meaning more BBQ and golf-club discussions around the next hot stock or investment idea. The boom in cryptocurrency speculation in 2020 was evidence of this. If your assets are generating enough income to meet your lifestyle needs, then who cares what everyone else is doing?

Bounce back

They say that the definition of resilience is the way in which you bounce back from setbacks or challenges that you face during your life. These challenges don't stop once you decide to retire; in fact, they tend to be more impactful. Life will constantly throw curveballs at you, with health and friendships often being the biggest areas of stress. On a darker note, retirement is a period in which you will all too regularly farewell long-term friends and family.

Looking at this from a financial perspective, things will always go wrong, but that's okay. Even the most successful fund managers get at least four out of every ten decisions wrong, but they still manage to deliver strong long-term returns for their investors. The key in both life and investing is to ensure that you don't compound challenging events by making the wrong decisions during period of heightened emotions.

Don't worry about money

All too often we hear stories about Peter or Greg at the local golf club being distraught because he has seen the price of X share fall during the day, or because Telstra has announced a cut to its dividend. Don't let this be you.

Retirement shouldn't be about tracking your investments every day or worrying about whether you will have enough dividends to pay for your groceries tomorrow. Money is a means to an end. It is a reward for your exertion across your career and should be used to enjoy experiences.

Use money to control your time, whether by outsourcing mundane tasks or simply enjoying the ability to do what you want, when you want. Don't let money control you; being controlled by your money can be the biggest drag on happiness.

Find your why

Anyone reading this book who was born after 1990 might be sick of hearing about Simon Sinek and his oft-quoted advice to 'find your why'. Unfortunately, he is right. You need to find your why; otherwise, the passing days will feel like an eternity.

Ask yourself, what are the things that bring you the most joy and engagement? It could be your children, or hiking, or travel, or cooking. If you don't know yet, that's also okay. How do you find it? Do you need to get out of your comfort zone and give some new things a try?

Bored of your partner's cooking? Take a pastry course. Want to build something? Look into woodworking. It could be as simple as trying to spend more time with your family, in which case, where you live will be central to this. Just don't fall into the routine of doing things that others want of you and not what brings your joy.

Become a bookworm

There is no better time than retirement to educate yourself. Now is not the time to rest on the laurels of your career or a lifetime in the workforce. Keeping your mind active in retirement has proven key to staving off dementia and ultimately lengthening your life.

Encouraging a healthy and inquisitive brain is essential to a long and successful retirement, but be wary of fixating too much on one thing. Too often we meet people who become obsessed with investments and trading, in many cases to their detriment. While a healthy interest in investments is a clear positive, don't let it rule your waking hours.

Think about trying a different newspaper or learning a new language. Maybe it's time to switch from non-fiction to fiction. Walk around a bookshop and buy some random books. You will be surprised by what you learn.

Take the stairs

While the benefits of being fit in your forties reverberate all the way into retirement, it is never too late to start. Ignore the posters of shredded 70-year-olds – this is simply unattainable to most people – and just stay active.

Always take the stairs. In retirement, your health should be your focus, as without it your ability to do the things you enjoy will be reduced substantially. It is more important than ever to take your health and diet seriously. Now is the time to get out and about more. Join those walking or fitness clubs, and find forms of exercise that you enjoy and that suit your schedule. Similarly, be wary of the long lunches and extra bottles of wine, and always make your regular check-ups with your doctor.

Discipline your way to success

It can take as long as two months for a behaviour to become a habit. Discipline is the way to success in retirement. Routine is central to good habits and supports strong mental health both before and during retirement.

Your need to work, commute and network helps build routine during your working life, but once this ends your routine naturally goes out the window. You don't need to plan every minute of every day, but simply consider locking in a few things every week that bring you structure. Having a schedule will allow you to maintain control of your own time. It will help to ensure that you don't fall into the 'bad routine' trap where your availability means that your movements are driven by others rather than by your own decisions. During quiet times, there is nothing more important than having something to look forward to.

Think beyond the grave

These final two rules are closely intertwined. Retirement is ultimately the time to focus on your legacy. It is normal to start thinking differently and bigger in retirement about what you want to leave to your family, friends and the world around you.

Legacy provides a true source of meaning to many, and getting your legacy right is all about engaging with your family and friends early. Is it financially driven? Does it have to be? Is it more about sharing skills, time or love with the next generation? Imparting knowledge and wisdom can be far more powerful than any inheritance or gift you are able to leave. This leads to our final note: ultimately, family is what truly matters.

Is life about the journey, or the destination? It's actually about the company and people you meet along the way.

You don't need to have children to have a family. Retirement is the time to spend meaningful periods with the people you love, put long-held grudges aside and look towards the future.

Action points

1. Write down three things, big or small, that you make you happy every week. It could be as simple as that first cup of coffee in the morning or walking your dog.
2. Book in some exercise for this week, next week and the rest of the month, whether that is a walk, a class or a bike ride.
3. Jump online and join a club to learn something new. It could be the University of the Third Age, Australian Shareholders' Association or even something more niche like French language classes.

Appendix
Investing in retirement

Among the biggest challenges, both emotionally and financially, of transitioning into retirement is the switch from receiving an 'active' income from exertion at work to relying on a 'passive' income generated by your investments. Having spent your lifetime seeing your super balance increase, retirement is the beginning of the reversal of this trend. For many, this feels unnatural and outright terrifying.

For the majority of retirees, retirement will extend across at least three decades and hence warrants a long-term view from even the most concerned investor. This appendix seeks to give you a foundation in the basics of investing and, at the very least, to provide some level of comfort with this difficult transition.

Put most simply, investing involves putting money into something that you believe will grow in value. There are three basic asset classes: cash, bonds and shares.

Cash needs no introduction – you use it to pay your bills and live your life. As for bonds and shares, thinking about your own family balance sheet offers a simple way to understand these. You may own your home or an investment property, in which case you are entitled to both the increase in value (capital growth) and any income generated from the property; this is equivalent to equity. You have likely funded the purchase of this asset via a loan from a bank, and in return you are paying both an amount of capital each month and interest at a certain rate. In this case, you have issued a 'bond' to the bank in return for a lump sum of capital.

This is a very simple start, but let's delve a little more deeply into these and a number of other types of assets.

Shares

Shares, or equities, are units of ownership in companies that trade on stock exchanges, such as the ASX. By owning a share in a business, you are entitled to the same portion of the profits that it generates in any given year. These profits are distributed to you in two ways: dividends and capital growth.

Capital growth, while not straightforward, comes from the increasing value of the company and thus the shares it has issued. This can be due to the increasing revenue or profit of said company or, alternatively, other people's perspectives on its growth prospects. Most companies reinvest a portion of their profits each year, increasing their value over time.

Dividends are a portion of company profits distributed to investors. They represent the excess profits that the company has chosen not to reinvest and has thus paid out to you as an investor.

While shares are generally considered riskier assets as share prices can fluctuate a great deal over the short term, they have shown a very strong track record of long-term growth. According to Vanguard, Australian shares (based on the S&P/ASX 200 index and its predecessor) have returned an average of 9.2 per cent a year over the 30 years to June 2023, well ahead of the return from

Australian listed property (7.3 per cent a year), Australian bonds (5.5 per cent a year) and cash (4.2 per cent a year). Australian shares also beat the return for international shares at 7.5 per cent a year; the only comparable asset class that did better than Australian shares was United States shares, which generated 10 per cent a year.

This way or that way?

There are two distinct ways you can invest into shares: by owning them directly – for example, by holding BHP in your super fund – or by pooling your money with other investors in the form of an exchange traded fund (ETF) or managed fund. Both options have their merits and drawbacks, which are generally determined your own comfort with and perspective on risk.

Australia is somewhat unique in that you can assume full control of the investment of your retirement savings. Whether through an industry fund or an SMSF, you can choose exactly how your funds are invested, down to the individual share or company, without the need for professional advice. This is fraught with both opportunity and danger.

On the one hand, buying into individual shares directly can lead to massive outperformance. To give just one example, CSL (the former Commonwealth Serum Laboratories) was floated on the Australian share market by its owner, the Australian Government, in June 1994 at the equivalent of 77 cents. Back then, it was the sole manufacturer of blood products in Australia and also had a substantial pharmaceuticals business. CSL was worth $292.4 million. At the time of writing, CSL is valued on the share market at $127 billion. It has made an investment return of 5515 per cent. (At its peak in February 2020 it was valued at more than $150 billion.) Along the share-price journey from 77 cents to $280,

CSL has consistently rewarded investors who buy it and watch it go higher.

Naturally, while things can go incredibly well, they can also do the opposite – just as some companies perform much better than the index over time, an awful lot don't. While some companies can magnify their shareholders' investment to a staggering degree, others can destroy it completely if they are mismanaged or simply fail to compete well enough in their business. Plenty of Australian investors are still scarred by the collapses of companies such as HIH Insurance, ABC Learning, Babcock & Brown, Allco, One.Tel and Harris Scarfe, all of which simply ran out of money and delisted, their shares becoming next to worthless.

The alternative to buying individual shares is the concept of 'pooling' assets with other investors. This allows you to invest in more assets and shares than you otherwise could if you were investing alone and, in addition, access professional management. Pooling comes in two forms, managed funds and ETFs, both of which ultimately do the same thing: combine your money with other people's to buy a diverse range of companies in which you own an equivalent share.

A managed fund, as the name suggests, is managed for you. Structured as a unit trust, your investment gives you an equivalent number of units, the value of which then changes based on the value of the underlying shares purchased. To sell or buy more of the fund, you must apply or redeem your units, at which point they will be repaid in cash. The alternative, an ETF, is by most measures the same structure but with one key difference: the units can be traded on a share market such as the ASX.

Buying shares directly increases both the risk and opportunity of outsized returns, whereas greater diversification via a pooled investment results in smoother returns and less bouncing around.

The active and passive options

This extends to a secondary question and consideration: the concept of active versus passive investing.

Investing is rare in that you are now able to receive the 'average' return, or that of the share market, for next to no cost; this is passive investing. Passive investing simply refers to (and has been facilitated by) the use of an index-tracking approach to investing. An 'index' is a particular portfolio of shares, such as the S&P/ASX200 or the S&P500. You hear daily updates on the performance of the larger indexes during news bulletins. Most indexes are constructed so that the largest companies on the share market, such as BHP in Australia or Apple overseas, receive the largest weightings within the index due to their relative importance. Thus, a passive fund simply buys these companies on your behalf at those weightings.

Active investing, on the other hand, is when you or a fund management company such as Platinum or Magellan seeks to use skill to choose individual shares that will perform better than the index. The fund manager hopes that its buying and selling activity will result in an overall portfolio performance that betters that of the index over a given period, and it will charge investors higher fees than a passive fund for that reason.

Beating the index over a given period is difficult, and it is even harder to repeat this success consistently over time. Standard and Poor's SPIVA reporting regularly highlights the fact that the vast majority of active strategies underperform the market (that is, the index) over the long term. Over any given period, there will be some active managers that beat the index, but it is not always the same ones.

Alpha and beta performance

Financial markets have evolved to the point that the index's return ('beta') has come to be thought of as the performance that investors have the right to expect. Active managers all say that they strive to beat the index (the return margin over that of the index is called 'alpha') and deliver alpha to justify their higher management fees, but they don't always manage to do it.

On the negative side, an investor in a passive, index-based fund will own all the stocks in that index – the duds as well as the stars. Passive investors know that they can never do better than the index. Many don't seem to mind this, especially if they have had negative experiences with active funds and their fees.

In practice, both passive and active approaches can play important roles in portfolios, particularly from the perspective of a retiree, and so both should be considered tools in the investor's kitbag. You don't need to choose between one (active investing) or the other (index-based funds held inside super or a brokerage account).

Franking credits

Australia is unique in that it has a dividend imputation system. This means that it acknowledges the amount of tax already paid by a company on profits that are then paid out as dividends to shareholders. The dividend is 'franked', such that when it is paid to shareholders, who must pay tax on it for a second time, the franking credit can be used to reduce said tax.

Here's how it works. First, a company pays taxes on its profits at the corporate tax rate. It then determines its taxable profits. The amount of tax paid by the company becomes the franking credit when the company distributes dividends to its shareholders – the company attaches the franking credit to the dividend payment. Companies can declare fully franked, partially franked (to any proportion) and unfranked dividends. The difference between fully franked and partially franked dividends comes down to the amount of franking credits that are attached to the dividends.

Franking credits are tax offsets that reduce the amount of income tax payable but ultimately seek to minimise double taxation. In other words, they are used to offset your individual tax liability, resulting in a lower overall tax bill (or increased refund). It means that you get to keep more of your income. If the franking credits exceed your tax liability, you may be eligible for a cash refund from the government. This means that you receive money back, providing you with additional income. These benefits make franking credits attractive to shareholders, particularly retirees or those in lower tax brackets.

For Australian resident investors, franking credits are the third element of total shareholder returns after capital gains and dividends. Over the long term, franking credits add about 1.4 to 1.5 per cent to the total return (capital gain plus dividends) from Australian shares.

International shares

Like investors of all nationalities, we have a natural 'home bias' towards companies we know well and do business with – think Woolies or Telstra. This is only strengthened by the franking 'free kick'. While that preference can be easily understood, Australian investors do need to diversify their investments outside of Australia, where most of the world's best and largest companies operate. This can be achieved through international ETFs, active funds or holding direct shares (which has become much easier over the last decade).

Establishing international diversification is vital for Australian investors for two main reasons. First, Australia represents less than 2 per cent of the global stock market by capitalisation. Second, the Australian stock market is highly concentrated at the top end: the top ten stocks account for just under half of the Australian market's benchmark index and are dominated by banking and resources stocks (although CSL, Wesfarmers and Woolworths are also there at the time of writing).

Australian investors should be looking to tap into industry exposures they cannot get in Australia to broaden the economic drivers that can be tailwinds for a share portfolio. For example, the Australian index is significantly underexposed to technology stocks, which make up just 6 per cent of the S&P/ASX 200 index compared with 28 per cent in the S&P500.

Diversifying into international shares is a must to ensure you have a share portfolio that is as efficient as possible in terms of capitalising on growth opportunities.

Cash and term deposits

Cash is both an asset class and a daily essential, as you use it to pay for goods and services. In its asset-class role, it is the bedrock of a portfolio in that it doesn't lose capital value and is highly accessible and liquid. Having a significant cash holding gives you the flexibility to readily take advantage of investment opportunities.

Cash includes bank deposits, term deposits, savings and cheque accounts, and cash management trusts. It suits those of us who have a short-term outlook or a low tolerance to risk, or at times when other asset classes are highly volatile. Cash provides a stable and low-risk income. However, the paradox of cash is that while it is the safest asset class, it cannot protect your assets from inflation.

In a term deposit, both the rate of return and the money you deposit is guaranteed: deposits of up to $250,000 are covered by the Australian Government under the Financial Claims Scheme should the financial institution your term deposit is with fail. However, recent experience, which saw the average Australian three-year term-deposit rate plunge to record lows, tells investors that term deposit rates shouldn't be considered static. Term deposits definitely have a role to play in the safety of a retirement portfolio, but they should not be the only things considered.

Bonds

Bonds, otherwise known as fixed-interest assets, sit near cash on the conservative side of the risk scale, but they are one of the most misunderstood assets despite their relatively simple structure.

Bonds are a loan: you lend money to a government or a company, and it guarantees to pay you interest on the due dates (at the 'coupon' rate) and pay back your principal (the face value) at maturity. The spectrum of bonds – from risk-free (if held to maturity) Commonwealth Government bonds, through semi-government bonds issued by the state governments, to corporate bonds – can offer a wide range of yields and thus fill a range of risk appetites.

Like term deposits, bonds have a known rate of return upfront, giving you certainty, and they also represent a legal obligation to the borrower. This makes bonds one of the few asset classes where you know what your returns will be over the life of the holding (if you know you will hold it to maturity).

When it comes to income, the critical difference between a bond and a share is that with a bond, the company must return to you interest and your principal when it says it will do so. With a share, there is no actual obligation on the company to pay a dividend. Share dividends can be reduced, or not paid at all, at the company's discretion.

Because of this greater certainty of income, bonds, like cash investments, are defensive assets that can protect your portfolio during tough times. Augmenting this quality is the fact that bonds generally perform differently to shares and have less volatility. Also, unlike term deposits, bonds are liquid – you can sell part of a holding at any time to fund cash requirements.

Hybrids

Sitting halfway between bonds and shares is a rare variety of assets called 'hybrid' securities. These are so named because they have characteristics of both equities (shares) and debt (bonds). They are issued by companies ranging from the nation's highest-rated banks to industrial companies without a credit rating. Using this range of issuers and the consequent range in yields, investors can put together portfolios that match the yield they are seeking with the risk they are prepared to bear.

Hybrids provide a cash yield from interest payments plus franking credits, which is the 'running yield'. It is usually based on a margin over a market rate at any time, similar to the way your mortgage is set.

Property

Property is also a major asset class in Australia, and a popular one at that. Investment property has long been part of the 'Great

Australian Dream', but the asset class spans well beyond that. Property as an investment can be split into residential, commercial and government, including:

- office property
- retail property
- industrial property
- hotels and other tourism property
- logistics property (such as warehouses, distribution centres and cold stores)
- data centres
- medical and other healthcare centres
- rural property
- petrol stations
- childcare centres
- storage facilities
- retirement accommodation.

There are many options to invest in property without the need to take out a mortgage to buy an investment property. These include ASX-listed real estate investment trusts (REITs) and unlisted vehicles ranging from property syndicates to multi-asset unlisted property funds. Beware of the latter, though, as much of this sector is unregulated.

Why invest in property? The key when seeking to transition from active to passive income is to ensure that the income is being delivered from multiple sources that are influenced by different factors. Property can at times be driven by very different trends to share markets, and it can provide a more consistent return in the form of rental income.

Alternatives

Alternative investments, often unknown to all but the most sophisticated investors, are not the traditional building blocks of a portfolio, namely shares, cash, bonds and property. As they have different returns streams from mainstream investments, alternatives are used to diversify an investment portfolio.

Alternatives can also have a low or even negative correlation to the traditional investments, so at times when all the traditional markets appear to fall at once, allocations to alternatives may fall to a much lesser extent (low correlation) or even move in the opposite direction (negative correlation). This ability to absorb shocks can take the risk out of portfolios. However, alternatives are not without risk.

The term 'alternative investments' is incredibly broad and complex but is usually considered to include:

- hedge funds, which are managed funds that can invest across many different markets and strategies with maximum flexibility, so they can make (or lose) money regardless of what the share and bond markets are doing
- managed futures and commodity trading adviser (CTA) strategies
- absolute-return equity-based funds, such as long-short funds, which will simultaneously go long (buy) under-valued stocks and short (sell) over-valued securities, and 'market-neutral' funds, which try to deliver above-market returns with lower risk by hedging out market risk, looking to negate the impact and risk of general market movements and trying to isolate the pure returns of individual stocks

- high-yield assets, such funds that invest in distressed debt, junk bonds and mezzanine debt
- commodities, such as precious and base metals, oil and energy, and soft (agricultural) commodities
- agribusiness, such as investment in forestry, farming or horticultural businesses
- cryptocurrencies (for example, Bitcoin and Ethereum) and other digital assets
- art and other collectible items, such as antiques, coins and wine.

The realm of alternative investments is beyond the scope of this book and in most cases is best considered with the support of a financial adviser.

Infrastructure and real assets

Real assets are physical assets that have an intrinsic worth due to their substance and properties. 'Real assets' mostly refers to property, infrastructure, agriculture and forestry, but it can also include commodities, equipment and natural resources. Real assets are usually considered for well-diversified portfolios because of their relatively low correlation with financial assets such as shares and bonds.

Infrastructure investments include physical assets such as transportation (rail, roads, tunnels, airports and ports), utilities, communication, and infrastructure for renewable energy and desalination and water treatment plants. It even includes social infrastructure such as affordable housing, aged care facilities, hospitals, prisons and courts. Infrastructure assets are long-term cash flow generators, with a high yield and, typically, little volatility. They are considered defensive investments, but this is not foolproof.

Like commercial property, infrastructure comes in listed and unlisted forms, with the same caveats. The volatility of the share market can mean the value of investments will fluctuate, making them higher risk. A benefit of listed infrastructure investments is that they are easier to sell and convert into cash. Unlisted infrastructure, on the other hand, may be less liquid and more difficult to trade.

Putting it all together

While it is all well and good to understand the major asset classes, the magic and challenge is in how you put them all together in the pursuit of your ultimate goal: generally a solid income or income and growth.

In financial adviser–speak, asset allocation is the process of dividing your investments among different asset classes, such as shares, bonds and cash. Asset allocation decisions are personal: the allocation that works best for you will change as you move through different times in your life, depending on how long you have to invest and your ability to tolerate risk. Your ideal asset allocation is the mix of investments, from most aggressive to safest, that will earn the best total return over time, tailored to your risk tolerance.

By investing in a variety of assets that are not closely correlated, investors can potentially earn reasonably predictable returns over the time period for which they need to invest, as opposed to if they were to invest in just one asset class, which would be too risky. Ultimately, you want the most efficient blend of assets that ensures you are not taking on more risk than necessary to deliver the outcome you seek.

Volatility

Asset allocation is incredibly important as it will help you deal with the most dreaded word in investing: 'volatility'.

In the investment world, 'volatility' refers to the fact that on some days, market indices and stock prices move up, and other days they move down. The more dramatic the swings, the higher the level of volatility and potential risk. Volatility is most challenging for retail investors (investors without professional support) as our psychological makeup means we tend to seek control during periods of stress, and investing is an emotional activity even for the calmest among us.

Volatility is often associated with big swings in either direction. For example, when the stock market rises or falls more than one per cent over a sustained period of time, it is called a 'volatile' market. Big landmark events, such as the election of US President Donald Trump and the British Brexit vote, can create a wave of increased volatility in markets. Volatility is always present in markets in terms of price action, but what has changed is that the speed of dissemination of information is far quicker than it was 20 years ago, people's ability to react quickly to that information has changed markets. At such times, the contribution of market participants – cash, equity or derivative instruments, high-frequency trading (HFT) or retail – can create a net effect that can be challenging for retail investors.

By spreading your portfolio across multiple asset classes, you are able to diversify the source of your returns and income as well as limiting the chance that you act irrationally during these periods of market stress.

Glossary

Allocated pension. A regular income stream when you retire that comes from your super.

Asset allocation. The process of buying investments across a range of different asset classes, such as shares, bonds and property.

Assets. Possessions, which may be expected to increase in value (such as property or shares) or lose value (such as cars). The *assets test* determines the value of your assets, which affects your eligibility for the age pension.

Bonds. When you loan money to a government or company in return for a guarantee that they will pay you interest on the due dates and the principal at maturity.

Business real property. Land and buildings used wholly and exclusively in a business.

Capital gains tax (CGT). The tax you pay on profits from disposing of assets.

Cash flow. Money coming in (income) or out (expenses). Positive cash flow is when more money is coming in than going out, and negative cash flow is when more money is going out than coming in.

Compounding. The repeated addition of interest payments to the principal, which causes the principal to grow exponentially as each new interest payment is added.

Contributions cap. The maximum amount you can contribute into your super each financial year.

Defensive assets. Assets that are expected to be less volatile, such as bonds and cash. They are generally less risky.

Discretionary expenses. Expenses that are not strictly essential. We call these 'capital' expenses as they contribute to greater enjoyment in your life, or 'investing in yourself'.

Diversification. Spreading your investments across a range of asset classes as well as a range of investments within each asset class.

Dividends. A portion of a corporation's profits that is paid out to shareholders.

Dollar cost averaging. The practice of investing a set dollar amount on a regular basis in order to smooth out share market fluctuations.

Equity. The value of your ownership of a property. For example, if you have a property valued at $600,000 and a mortgage of $400,000, then you have $200,000 or 40 per cent equity in that property.

Exchange-traded fund (ETF). A basket of securities that tracks or seeks to outperform an underlying index.

Franking credits. Tax credits paid by corporations to their shareholders along with dividend payments. They aim to reduce or eliminate double taxation, since the corporation has already paid tax on the dividends they distribute to shareholders. They are also known as 'imputation credits'.

Growth assets. Assets that are expected to generate higher returns over the long term, such as shares and property. However, they are also higher risk.

Home Equity Access Scheme (HEAS). A scheme that lets eligible older Australians use the equity in their home (or other Australian real estate) to access fortnightly loan payments from the Australian Government to a maximum of 150 per cent of the maximum fortnightly rate of age pension.

Home reversion or equity release arrangement. An arrangement whereby you sell off a share of the future value of your home in exchange for cash.

Index. A group of financial instruments (such as shares) that represents and measures the performance of a specific market, asset class, sector or investment strategy.

Lifecycle investing. An investing approach whereby you take on more investment risk when you are younger to aim for higher investment returns, then shift focus towards defensive assets as you approach retirement to preserve your capital.

Liquidity. The ability to quickly and easily convert assets into cash.

Longevity risk. The risk that you will outlive your savings.

Meme stocks. Shares that have gained popularity through social media and which online communities actively follow and trade.

MySuper. Superannuation products that are not allowed to charge entry fees, hidden fees or commissions to financial advisers. In 2013 they replaced existing default funds for all funds that met the MySuper standards.

Passive income. Money you did not have to trade your time to earn, such as rental income from an investment property.

Preservation age. The age at which you can access your super.

Pretirement. The period before retirement – beginning in your late fifties or even earlier – when you begin to decide when and how you will retire.

Principal. The value of the initial investment.

Rebalancing. Buying and/or selling assets in your portfolio with the aim of ensuring that your asset allocation remains aligned with your investment goals and risk profile.

Retirement income covenant. Legislation that requires superannuation trustees of funds regulated by APRA to have a retirement income strategy that outlines how they plan to assist their members in retirement.

Retirement standard. ASFA's assessment of the annual income required to fund retirement. It has two tiers: 'modest' and 'comfortable'.

Reverse mortgage. A loan that uses the equity in your home as security.

Salary sacrificing. When you ask your employer to pay part of your pre-tax salary into your super account. The payments are also called 'concessional contributions'; 'non-concessional contributions' are when you make voluntary super contributions from your after-tax pay.

Self-managed superannuation fund (SMSF). A private super fund that you manage yourself: you choose the investments and the insurance. When you retire, it pays you a pension.

Superannuation guarantee (SG). The minimum amount of super an employer must pay in addition to an employee's wages.

Timing the market. Moving in and out of investments based on what you think those investments will do in the short term.

Transition to Retirement (TTR). Provisions that endorse the ability for individuals to transition to retirement by reducing their work hours or shifting to a less demanding role in the later years of their careers.

Volatility. The unpredictable and sometimes sharp rises and falls in the price of assets.

Wholesale investor. Otherwise known as a 'sophisticated' investor, they are someone who can certify that they earn $250,000 a year or have more than $2.5 million in net assets. They can access investment opportunities that 'retail' investors cannot, but they lose some rights in return.

About the authors

Jamie Nemtsas and Drew Meredith are co-founders of Wattle Partners, a specialist fee-for-service financial advisory firm that focuses solely on retirement. They are both SMSF Specialist Advisors.

Jamie has founded several businesses in financial services and marketing, and has a unique skillset in helping business owners deal with the difficult transition to earning a passive income. He has a bachelor's degree in banking and finance and a postgraduate diploma in financial planning, and served as president and board member of the Australian Investors Association (AIA), a non-profit association that seeks to support greater financial literacy.

Drew's career has been spent providing financial advice, specialising in superannuation, SMSFs and investments. Drew is co-host of *The Australian Investors Podcast*, the leading personal investment podcast in Australia, and is a regular contributor to trade and mainstream news publications. He has a bachelor's degree in commerce and a postgraduate diploma in financial planning. He provides regular support to the AIA, the Australian Shareholder's Association and the University of the Third Age, among others.

References

Chapter 1: The long road that is retirement

Australian Bureau of Statistics (ABS), 'Retirement and Retirement Intentions, Australia', 2020-21, accessed 22 January 2024, abs.gov.au/statistics/labour/employment-and-unemployment/retirement-and-retirement-intentions-australia/latest-release.

Vanguard, 'Vanguard Digital Index Chart', accessed 23 January 2024, insights.vanguard.com.au/VolatilityIndexChart/ui/advisor.html.

Hume, Senator the Hon. Jane, 'Release of retirement income covenant exposure draft', media release, 27 September 2021, parlinfo.aph.gov.au/parlInfo/search/display/display.w3p;query=Id%3A%22media%2Fpressrel%2F8197298%22;src1=sm1.

Australian Securities & investments Commission (ASIC), 'Review finds super trustees need to improve retirement outcomes planning', media release, 18 July 2023, asic.gov.au/about-asic/news-centre/find-a-media-release/2023-releases/23-191mr-review-finds-super-trustees-need-to-improve-retirement-outcomes-planning.

Australian Institute of Health and Welfare (AIHW), 'Physical activity', updated 19 May 2023, aihw.gov.au/reports/physical-activity/physical-activity.

AIHW, 'Impact of physical inactivity as a risk factor for chronic conditions: Australian Burden of Disease', 22 November 2017, aihw.gov.au/reports/burden-of-disease/impact-of-physical-inactivity-chronic-conditions/summary.

Beyond Blue, 'Look after your mental health and wellbeing', accessed 22 January 2024, beyondblue.org.au/mental-health/wellbeing.

Chapter 2: When to retire?

ABS, op. cit.

ABS, 'Counts of Australian Businesses, including Entries and Exits', July 2019 – June 2023, accessed 22 January 2024, abs.gov.au/statistics/ economy/business-indicators/counts-australian-businesses-including-entries-and-exits/latest-release.

ABS 'Labour Force, Australia', December 2023, accessed 22 January 2024, abs.gov.au/statistics/labour/employment-and-unemployment/ labour-force-australia/latest-release.

Australian Law Reform Commission (ALRC), 'Accessing superannuation', 8 April 2013, alrc.gov.au/publication/access-all-ages-older-workers-and-commonwealth-laws-alrc-report-120/8-superannuation-2/accessing-superannuation/.

Stine-Morrow, EAL, Parisi, JM, Morrow, DG & Park, DC, 'The effects of an engaged lifestyle on cognitive vitality: A field experiment', *Psychology and Aging*, vol. 23, no. 4, 2008, pp. 778–786.

Chapter 3: How much is enough?

Australian Super, 'Retire with confidence', accessed 22 January 2024, australiansuper.com/campaigns/confident-retirement-planning.

The Association of Superannuation Funds of Australia (ASFA), *ASFA Retirement Standard*

Detailed budget breakdowns, September quarter 2023, superannuation.asn.au/resources/retirement-standard/.

Moneysmart, 'How much super you need', accessed 22 January 2024, moneysmart.gov.au/grow-your-super/how-much-super-you-need.

Commonwealth of Australia, *Intergenerational Report 2023: Australia's future to 2063*, 24 August 2023, treasury.gov.au/publication/2023-intergenerational-report.

National Seniors Australia and Challenger, *The cost of living and older Australians' financial wellbeing*, September 2023, nationalseniors.com. au/research/finances/financial-wellbeing-and-the-cost-of-living.

National Seniors Australia and Challenger, *The evolution of retirement income: A 2022 snapshot*, August 2022, nationalseniors.com.au/uploads/Final-Challenger-report-22.8.22.pdf.

Chapter 4: Build your team of experts

Cambridge Business English Dictionary, 'financial literacy', accessed 22 January 2024, dictionary.cambridge.org/dictionary/english/financial-literacy.

Australian Competition & Consumer Commission (ACCC), 'National Anti-Scam Centre', accessed 22 January 2024, accc.gov.au/national-anti-scam-centre.

Commonwealth of Australia. *National Financial Capability Strategy*, February 2022, files.moneysmart.gov.au/media/vyfbpg4x/national-financial-capability-strategy-2022.pdf.

Fidelity International, *Building better retirement futures*, accessed 22 January 2024, fidelity.com.au/sites/fidelity/assets/File/Fidelity%20-%20Retirement%20Investing%20Report_FINAL.pdf.

Fidelity International, 'The value of advice', accessed 22 January 2024, fidelity.com.au/insights/investment-articles/the-value-of-advice/.

ACCC, 'ACCC calls for united front as scammers steal over $3bn from Australians', media release, 17 April 2023, accc.gov.au/media-release/accc-calls-for-united-front-as-scammers-steal-over-3bn-from-australians.

Financial Adviser Standards and Ethics Authority Ltd, *Financial Planners and Advisers Code of Ethics 2019*, 8 February 2019, asic.gov.au/for-finance-professionals/afs-licensees/professional-standards-for-financial-advisers/code-of-ethics.

Adviser Ratings, *2023 Australian Financial Advice Landscape*, accessed 22 January 2024, app.hubspot.com/documents/5373226/view/507378549?accessId=178a05.

Dew, L, 'Advice fees rise 40 per cent in five years', *Money Management*, 13 April 2023, adviserratings.com.au/media/advice-fees-rise-40-per-cent-in-five-years.

National Heart Foundation of Australia, 'Benefits of walking', accessed 22 January 2024, walking.heartfoundation.org.au/benefits.

Avramova, N, 'Friends and family may help Italians live healthier and longer', *CNN*, updated 9 May 2019, edition.cnn.com/2019/05/09/health/social-connections-health-benefits-intl/index.html.

Huang, AR et al., 'Social isolation and 9-year dementia risk in community-dwelling Medicare beneficiaries in the United States', *Journal of the American Geriatrics Society*, vol. 71, no. 3, March 2023, pp. 765–773.

Chapter 5: Future-proofing and estate planning

Gruber, J, 'Australians unprepared for $3.5 trillion wealth transfer' *Firstlinks*, 25 October 2023, firstlinks.com.au/australians-unprepared-35tn-dollar-wealth-transfer.

Wise, J, 'If you don't, who will? 12 million Australians have no estate plans', *Finder*, 29 November 2022, finder.com.au/australians-have-no-estate-plans.

ABS, 'Marriages and Divorces, Australia', 2022, accessed 22 January 2024, abs.gov.au/statistics/people/people-and-communities/marriages-and-divorces-australia/latest-release.

Chapter 6: Tax and super do the heavy lifting

ASFA, *Superannuation Statistics*, September 2023 superannuation.asn.au/resources/super-stats/.

Drury, B, 'Super fund performance: Monthly returns to December 2023', *SuperGuide*, updated 18 January 2024, superguide.com.au/comparing-super-funds/investment-performance-latest-super-returns.

Read, M, 'Super sector hits $3.3trn as retail funds turn the corner', *The Australian Financial Review*, 24 August 2021, afr.com/policy/economy/super-sector-hits-3-3trn-as-retail-funds-turn-the-corner-20210824-p58lfb.

The Australian Prudential Regulation Authority, 'APRA releases superannuation statistics for September 2023', media release, 21 November 2023, apra.gov.au/quarterly-superannuation-statistics.

Australian Taxation Office (ATO), 'Appoint your trustees or directors', updated 25 September 2023, ato.gov.au/individuals-and-families/ super-for-individuals-and-families/self-managed-super-funds-smsf/ setting-up-an-smsf/appoint-your-trustees-or-directors.

ATO, 'Thinking about self-managed super', updated 11 January 2023, ato.gov.au/individuals-and-families/super-for-individuals-and-families/ self-managed-super-funds-smsf/thinking-about-an-smsf.

Chapter 7: Retirement-focused investment strategies

Rusell Investments, 'The 15/30/50 Retirement Lifestyle Rule', blog, 9 May 2019, russellinvestments.com/uk/blog/the-retirement-lifestyle-rule.

Chapter 8: Free kicks

ATO, 'Super co-contribution', updated 2 August 2023, ato.gov.au/individuals-and-families/super-for-individuals-and-families/ super/growing-and-keeping-track-of-your-super/how-to-save-more-in-your-super/government-super-contributions/super-co-contribution.

ATO, 'Stapled super funds', updated 1 November 2021, ato.gov.au/ businesses-and-organisations/super-for-employers/stapled-super-funds.

Class, 'Class launches 2023 Annual Benchmark Report', media release, 13 September 2023, class.com.au/news/class-launches-2023-annual-benchmark-report/.

Chapter 9: Managing market anxiety

National Seniors Australia and Challenger, *The cost of living and older Australians' financial wellbeing*, September 2023, nationalseniors.com. au/research/finances/financial-wellbeing-and-the-cost-of-living.

Vanguard, '2023 Vanguard Index Chart', accessed 22 January 2024, vanguard.com.au/personal/support/index-chart.

Markowitz, H, 'Portfolio Selection', *The Journal of Finance*, vol. 7, no. 1, March 1952, pp. 77–91.

Wolcott, I & Hughes, J, *Towards understanding the reasons for divorce*, Australian Institute of Family Studies, June 1999, aifs.gov.au/research/ research-reports/towards-understanding-reasons-divorce.

Chapter 10: The mistakes we make

Commonwealth of Australia. *National Financial Capability Strategy*, February 2022, files.moneysmart.gov.au/media/vyfbpg4x/national-financial-capability-strategy-2022.pdf.

Treasury Laws Amendment (Putting Members' Interests First) Bill 2019

Lewis, M, *The Big Short: Inside the doomsday machine*, W.W. Norton, 2011.

Osman, M, 'Change Your Ways: How Long Does It Take To Form a Habit?', blog, *HubSpot*, 5 July 2023, blog.hubspot.com/the-hustle/how-long-does-it-take-to-form-a-habit.

Vanguard, '2023 Vanguard Index Chart', accessed 22 January 2024, vanguard.com.au/personal/support/index-chart.

Housel, M, *The Psychology of Money: Timeless lessons on wealth, greed, and happiness*, Harriman House, Petersfield, UK, 2020.

Campbell, K, *Buying Happiness: Learn to invest your time and money better*, Major Street Publishing, Melbourne, 2023.

Lucas, E, *Mind over Money: Why understanding your money behaviour will improve your financial freedom*, revised edition, Major Street Publishing, 2024.

Appendix: Investing in retirement

Yahoo! Finance, 'CSL Limited (CSL.AX)', accessed 22 January 2024, au.finance.yahoo.com/quote/CSL.AX/history.

deListed Australia, accessed 22 January 2024, delisted.com.au.

Ganti, AR, Stoddart, G & di Giola, D, *SPIVA® Australia Scorecard*, S&P Dow Jones Indices, 12 September 2023, spglobal.com/spdji/en/spiva/article/spiva-australia/.

Francis, S, 'How franking has boosted your returns', *InvestSMART*, 18 March 2009, investsmart.com.au/investment-news/how-franking-has-boosted-your-returns/64291.

Index

Work With Jamie and Drew

Jamie and Drew are financial advisers and the directors of Wattle Partners, a specialist financial advice company focused on retirement.

Wattle Partners' services include:

- building a personalised retirement strategy focused on providing you with a passive income
- advice on the best portfolio of investments to suit your personal position and objectives
- managing superannuation, personal and other investment portfolios on your behalf of clients
- advice on superannuation strategy, including self-managed super funds, contributions and pensions
- strategies to help navigate the transition from a salary or small-business sale into a retirement-focused income.

Find out more about how Jamie and Drew can work with you and your family:

wattlepartners.com.au
adviser@wattlepartners.com.au
03 8414 2901

For regular insights, follow Jamie, Drew and Wattle Partners:

linkedin.com/in/jamienemtsas
linkedin.com/in/drew-meredith-88aba620
linkedin.com/company/wattlepartners
youtube.com/channel/UCaYh3o2CrQOv5aMP-Pny8mA
raskmedia.com.au/podcasts/australian-investors-podcast

Be better with
business books

MAJOR STREET

We hope you enjoy reading this book. We'd love you to post
a review on social media or your favourite bookseller site.
Please include the hashtag #majorstreetpublishing.

Major Street Publishing specialises in business, leadership,
personal finance and motivational non-fiction books. If you'd
like to receive regular updates about new Major Street books,
email info@majorstreet.com.au and ask to be added to our
mailing list.

Visit majorstreet.com.au to find out more about our books
(print, audio and ebooks) and authors, read reviews and find
links to our Your Next Read podcast.

We'd love you to follow us on social media.

in linkedin.com/company/major-street-publishing
f facebook.com/MajorStreetPublishing
⊙ instagram.com/majorstreetpublishing
𝕏 @MajorStreetPub